OFFSHORE LANDS

fm

OFFSHORE LANDS

Oil and Gas Leasing and Conservation on the Outer Continental Shelf

WALTER J. MEAD

ASBJORN MOSEIDJORD

DENNIS D. MURAOKA

PHILIP E. SORENSEN

Foreword by
Stephen L. McDonald

Pacific Studies in Public Policy
PACIFIC INSTITUTE FOR PUBLIC POLICY RESEARCH
San Francisco, California

ISBN 0-936488-01-8 (paper)
    0-936488-10-7 (cloth)

Library of Congress Catalog Card Number 85-63548

Printed in the United States of America

Pacific Institute for Public Policy Research
177 Post Street
San Francisco, California 94108

Library of Congress Cataloging in Publication Data

Offshore lands.

  (Pacific studies in public policy)
  Bibliography: p.
  Includes index.
  1. Oil and gas leases—United States. 2. Continental shelf—
United States. 3. Offshore oil industry—Government policy—
United States. 4. Offshore gas industry—Government policy—
United States. I. Mead, Walter J. II. Series.
HD242.5.034   1985   333.8'23'0973   85-63548
ISBN 0-936488-10-7 (alk. paper)
ISBN 0-936488-01-8 (pbk. : alk. paper)

PACIFIC INSTITUTE

FOR PUBLIC POLICY RESEARCH

The Pacific Institute for Public Policy Research is an independent, tax-exempt research and educational organization. The Institute's program is designed to broaden public understanding of the nature and effects of market processes and government policy.

With the bureaucratization and politicization of modern society, scholars, business and civic leaders, the media, policymakers, and the general public have too often been isolated from meaningful solutions to critical public issues. To facilitate a more active and enlightened discussion of such issues, the Pacific Institute sponsors in-depth studies into the nature of and possible solutions to major social, economic, and environmental problems. Undertaken regardless of the sanctity of any particular government program, or the customs, prejudices, or temper of the times, the Institute's studies aim to ensure that alternative approaches to currently problematic policy areas are fully evaluated, the best remedies discovered, and these findings made widely available. The results of this work are published as books and monographs, and form the basis for numerous conference and media programs.

Through this program of research and commentary, the Institute seeks to evaluate the premises and consequences of government policy, and provide the foundations necessary for constructive policy reform.

PACIFIC STUDIES IN PUBLIC POLICY

RESOLVING THE HOUSING CRISIS
Government Policy, Decontrol, and the Public Interest
Edited with an Introduction by M. Bruce Johnson

OFFSHORE LANDS
Oil and Gas Leasing and Conservation on the Outer Continental Shelf
By Walter J. Mead, et al.
Foreword by Stephen L. McDonald

ELECTRIC POWER
Deregulation and the Public Interest
Edited by John C. Moorhouse
Foreword by Harold Demsetz

TAXATION AND THE DEFICIT ECONOMY
Fiscal Policy and Capital Formation in the United States
Edited by Dwight R. Lee
Foreword by Michael J. Boskin

THE AMERICAN FAMILY AND THE STATE
Edited by Joseph R. Peden and Fred R. Glahe
Foreword by Robert Nisbet

DEALING WITH DRUGS
Problems of Government Control
Edited by Ronald Hamowy

CRISIS AND LEVIATHAN
Critical Episodes in the Growth of American Government
By Robert Higgs
Foreword by Arthur A. Ekirch, Jr.

FORTHCOMING

THE NEW CHINA
Comparative Economic Development in Hong Kong, Taiwan, and Mainland China

POLITICAL BUSINESS CYCLES
The Economics and Politics of Stagflation

RATIONING HEALTH CARE
Medical Licensing in the United States

CRIME, POLICE, AND THE COURTS

MYTH AND REALITY IN SOCIAL WELFARE

HEALTH CARE DELIVERY INSTITUTIONS

RENT CONTROL IN SANTA MONICA

HEALTH INSURANCE: PUBLIC AND PRIVATE

UNEMPLOYMENT AND THE STATE

For further information on the Pacific Institute's program and a catalog of publications, please contact:

PACIFIC INSTITUTE FOR PUBLIC POLICY RESEARCH
177 Post Street
San Francisco, California 94108

CONTENTS

LIST OF FIGURES

LIST OF TABLES

FOREWORD

On behalf of all the people of the United States, the federal government possesses nearly a billion acres of land on the Outer Continental Shelf (OCS). The geology of much of this land is suitable to the formation of oil and gas deposits. The U.S. Geological Survey estimates that there may be as much as 40 billion barrels of oil and 230 trillion cubic feet of gas, economically producible, remaining to be discovered on the OCS.[1] Thus far, only about 5 percent of the area has been offered for lease, and only about half of that has actually been leased.[2] Although the Reagan administration has accelerated the schedule for leasing, it will probably be many decades before the full potential for leasing is exhausted. Thus it is not too late to reap substantial benefits from an appropriate leasing policy.

The leasing of public lands to private firms for oil and gas exploration, development, and production raises a number of policy issues. What should be the objective(s) of leasing? How should the lands be chosen for periodic offering? What should be the rate of leasing? Assuming competitive bidding for leases, what should be the bid basis—lease bonus, royalty rate, profit share, or other? How can the government be assured

1. Comptroller General of the United States, *Issues in Leasing Offshore Lands for Oil and Gas Development,* EMD-81-59 (Washington, D.C.: General Accounting Office, 1981), p. 5.
2. Ibid., pp. 1–3.

of effective competition in bidding, so that it tends to receive fair market value for the leases it grants? What diligence requirements should there be? What safeguards should there be for conservation and environmental protection? To these and other questions, the present volume offers answers based on sound economic principles and skillful empirical investigation. The result is a major contribution to the literature on OCS leasing, one that is accessible to the general public as well as the professional reader.

At the heart of any discussion of this subject is the concept of economic rent. In the present context, economic rent is the surplus that oil and gas lands yield over the necessary costs of exploration, development, and production, including a normal competitive return on investment. (Marginal land yields only costs plus normal return—a zero surplus.) It is therefore the value that knowledgeable competitive bidders would tend to offer for the right to explore, develop, and produce for profit on a given tract of land. The payment of this surplus to the landowner in no way reduces the supply of oil and gas, since there remains enough revenue to cover necessary costs and normal return, even on the marginal tracts of land. Thus, as a first approximation, it can be said that the government should seek to capture all of the economic rent available, no more and no less.

At the time of leasing, which takes place after some predrilling exploration but before drilling an exploratory well, the amount of economic rent available from a tract cannot be known with certainty. Competitive operators may therefore bid more or less than the full economic rent available on a given tract. But if operators systematically bid too little, then competition and new entry will tend to raise typical bids; if they bid too much, competition and exit will cause typical bids to fall. Thus, in the long run and over all tracts, competitive bidders will tend to bid the actual economic rent, and they will tend to earn no more and no less than a normal rate of return, adjusted for risk and uncertainty. As the reader will see in Chapter 3, this principle is the basis of the authors' evaluation of the adequacy of bonus bidding.

There is another relevant principle. Rent may be paid at any time in the leasable "life" of a tract. Under bonus bidding, it is paid in a lump sum before exploratory drilling begins; under royalty bidding, it is paid as oil and gas are produced, down to the day of abandonment. To make streams of payment comparable, they must be discounted to the present at a rate reflecting the cost of capital, with a risk and uncertainty premium. A competitive bonus would be calculated as the up-front lump-sum payment that would make the present value of expected cash flow equal to zero, where revenues are positive cash flows, expenses are negative cash flows, and the normal rate of return is embodied in the discount factor. Similarly, a royalty bid would be calculated as the stream of production payments, expressed as a share of output, that would make the present value of expected cash flow equal to zero.[3] Presumably an operator would not be partial to either of two streams of payment having the same present value, even if undiscounted values are different. Likewise, government as landowner is presumably neutral as to streams of receipts that have the same present value. Rationally, it should seek the stream of receipts of true rent that has the highest present value, not necessarily the highest undiscounted value.

This last point has three implications worthy of mention here. First, government as landowner may, under some circumstances, prefer later receipts to earlier ones. Suppose that the government employs a lower rate of discount than do oil and gas operators because, unlike operators, government is not subject to ruin in the leasing-production process. A lease bonus would reflect some operator's rate of discount. A royalty or profit share having the same present value to an operator would have a greater present value to government as landowner if the latter employs a lower rate of discount. As the authors of this book point out, however, there is a loss of efficiency with royalty bidding; thus, even with a lower rate of discount, government may prefer to grant leases on the basis of lease bonus. Furthermore, as noted above, because of lower risk, operators may discount royalty payments at a lower rate than bonus payments; hence there may be a smaller discrepancy between present value to operators and present value to government.

Second, because of the relevance of discounting, it is in the interest of government as landowner on behalf of society to lease the most valuable (rent-rich) prospects first. Other things being the same, shifting rents from the future toward the present enhances present value. One way of doing that is to lease rich deposits early and poor deposits later. This point argues, generally, for careful selection of lands to be offered for lease and against areawide leasing in which prospects of widely varying quality are offered together. Moreover, it reinforces the consideration that operators tend to select the better prospects first and will have explored them (through predrilling) more thoroughly at the time of leasing.

Third—again, other things being the same—government can secure

---

3. Because the risk is smaller in royalty bidding, operators may employ a lower rate of discount in deriving present value.

more present value by rapid, as opposed to slow, leasing. It does not follow that a sudden, unexpected acceleration of leasing would be desirable, for then other important things are not likely to be equal. Specifically, predrilling exploration would be less complete, uncertainty and discount rates would be greater, competition in bidding would be more limited, capital funds for leasing would be more restricted, and the availability of equipment and critical personnel would be less ample. In short, government is more likely to lose present value of rents than to gain it. If a faster rate of leasing is desirable, it should be approached gradually, with full announcement of intent and with a view to sufficient sustainability to justify an increase in the industry's capacity to explore. develop, produce, and transport. Lack of sustainability suggests a boom-and-bust cycle of activity and a probable long-run loss of rent.

Among the many contributions of this book, one stands out prominently: the observation, arrived at theoretically and supported empirically, that lease bonus bidding is superior to other systems of leasing. It has some theoretical drawbacks, but the empirical evidence suggests that they are not very important.

Bonus bidding has several distinctive characteristics. First, since the bonus is an up-front payment, and often a large one, participation in bidding requires more initial capital than it does in other systems. Greater capital requirements may restrict competition, particularly by small firms just entering the industry, or effectively require them to participate in joint bidding arrangements. The capital requirements and anticompetitive effects may be severe if the government as lessor offers all its lands for lease within a short period of time.

Second, bonus bidding maximizes risk- or uncertainty-bearing by the lessee and minimizes the sharing of risk by the lessor. The additional negative cash flow at the beginning of the production cycle, where uncertainty is great, clearly increases the dispersion of possible outcomes. This dispersion of possible outcomes repels capital, reduces competition, and raises the effective discount rate employed by prospective lessees.

Third, and this is clearly a positive factor, bonus bidding requires a payment that, once made, becomes a sunk cost irrelevant to subsequent exploration, development, production, and abandonment decisions. Rational economic decisions are based on the present value of expected net cash flow from the point of decision and onward. Thus, if exploratory drilling reveals a deposit that promises to yield a normal or better rate of return only on development investment, development and production should occur even though there is a loss on the total investment, including lease bonus and exploratory drilling. Similarly, abandonment should not occur until the present value of expected net cash flow from production falls below the salvage value of production equipment, regardless of the rate of return on development investment. In each case, activity goes forward if that activity pays for itself and possibly contributes even the smallest amount to the recovery of previously sunk costs. In each case, the operator makes himself better off than with premature abandonment.

It is difficult to overstate the importance of this last point. The up-front, sunk-cost nature of the lease bonus payment is a major contributor to the efficiency of the oil and gas industry. With it more discoveries are developed and more production occurs before abandonment than with alternative rent payments. Not only is there incentive to operators, but the results are beneficial from a social point of view. Each activity is pursued to the point where the last increment to output just pays for itself. Moreover, leases tend to go to firms that are most efficient in all phases of the industry, and each firm has the incentive to minimize cost after leasing because it needs to share a minimum of cost-saving with a passive lessor.

In contrast to bonus bidding, royalty bidding requires no up-front payment to secure a lease (other than the usual nominal bonus). It therefore requires less capital than does bonus bidding. This in turn tends to increase freedom of entry and competition in bidding. It puts less of a premium on joint bidding by small firms. It poses less of a problem in ensuring competition and fair value return when leasing is accelerated.

In addition, royalty bidding is a way of shifting some risk from the lessee to the lessor. It results in a smaller dispersion of possible outcomes to the former, and a larger one to the latter. This suggests that lessees will employ a lower rate of discount than under bonus bidding, and the government as lessor a higher one.

Finally, and highly important, whereas the bonus is a sunk cost during development and production, the royalty is a current, variable cost that affects decisions regarding development, production, and abandonment. Thus, if a marginal discovery is made, a high prospective royalty reduces the likelihood that development and production will pay for themselves from the lessee's point of view. Similarly, with a high royalty to pay, operators will find that the degree of depletion will not be as great when the present value of expected net cash flow falls below the salvage value of the producing equipment. The higher the royalty, the more premature is abandonment from a social point of view. In contrast to a bonus, a royalty may be thought of as an artificial production cost—artificial in the sense that it is intended to recover a surplus over actual costs but acts as if it were one of the actual costs of labor and capital. As an artificial cost, it induces lessees to take uneconomic action, such as underdevelopment of discoveries and premature abandonment of producing deposits.

Since bonus bidding and royalty bidding have their respective advantages and disadvantages, it is impossible on purely theoretical grounds to say that one is superior to the other. That is where the empirical work reported in this volume comes in. Suppose that bonus bidding, because of the necessity of an up-front payment, significantly reduces competition in securing leases. We would then expect to find that those actually securing leases would earn above average rates of return on those leases, paying less than the full economic rent on them. If, on the other hand, bonus bidding has no significant anticompetitive effects, those securing leases should earn only a normal rate of return, paying on average the full economic rent for those leases. The actual rate of return is, of course, an empirical question.

Using the U.S. Geological Survey's Lease Production and Revenue data bases, the authors compute the rate of return on over a thousand OCS leases issued in the Gulf of Mexico from 1954 through 1969, all involving a bonus bid. The computed average rate of return after taxes is 10.7 percent. This compares with an average rate of return on stockholders' equity of 11.7 percent for all manufacturing corporations in the United States, 1954–1983. If the latter figure may be taken as a competitive normal rate of return on investment for the period, it can be stated that lease bonus bidding on the OCS gave results fully consistent with competition and complete capture of economic rent. Apparently the theoretical anticompetitive effects of bonus bidding are not practically significant. It is likely that joint bidding by smaller companies overcomes capital- and risk-constraints and results in more, not less, competition. Thus, on both theoretical and empirical grounds, lease bonus bidding turns out to be a highly satisfactory method of granting oil and gas leases on the OCS. This conclusion is reinforced by an analysis in which high bids are regressed on a number of relevant variables.

The authors also review the empirical evidence concerning alternatives to lease bonus bidding, particularly royalty bidding and profit share bidding. This evidence, chiefly in regard to efficiency and compliance costs, further supports the view that lease bonus bidding is superior. Indeed, one of the principal disadvantages of profit share bidding is the high cost of monitoring financial records and enforcing efficient operations.

The empirical findings in this book are remarkable in at least two ways. First, those with regard to rate of return are unique in their coverage and thorough analysis. Second, the impact of the findings is all the greater in view of the great variation in costs, prices, and tax rates in the study period. The tendency toward a normal rate of return despite this variation speaks strongly for the continuous presence of active competition in the OCS oil and gas industry. Furthermore, it strongly suggests that bidders have more knowledge and foresight than the term *uncertainty* implies. They can indeed estimate prospective economic rent with some accuracy—not complete accuracy, of course—in advance of exploratory drilling. Knowledge, competition, and reaction to error tend to assure that government as lessor receives all the economic rent.

Other issues in OCS leasing, such as diligence requirements or the assurance of expeditious development of leases, are considered in Chapter 5. Government is concerned about diligence for a number of reasons, ranging from early reduction of import dependence to prompt receipt of rent payments in order to maximize present value. Generally, diligence is not a significant problem when leases are granted on the basis of bonus bid. When an operator has had to make a large up-front payment to secure a lease, he loses interest and reduces rate of return every day of delay in developing the lease and beginning production. It is in his economic interest to develop and produce promptly. Under royalty bidding or profit share bidding, in contrast, the up-front payment is nominal, and substantial rent payments begin only with production. There is little motivation to develop and produce promptly. Indeed, under these types of bidding there is motivation to secure a lease and hold it for speculative purposes in the hope of a price rise, a tax reduction, or the like. Diligence can only be assured by short primary lease terms and administrative monitoring of activities once development begins. For another reason, then, bonus bidding is a superior method of leasing.

The authors of this study rightly consider that oil and gas conservation is one of the aims of government, in leasing as well as production regulation. In this connection, conservation may be defined as a manner—and time distribution—of production that maximizes the present value of the resource to society. Continuous conservation calls not only for the prevention of physical wastes (when cost effective), but also for shifts in the time distribution of production whenever there is a change in the rate of interest or a change in the relation of expected future prices and costs to present prices and costs. For example, a rise in the rate of interest calls for a shift in production toward the present; a rise in expected future prices relative to present ones calls for a shift in production toward the future. We have seen that bonus bidding is neutral with respect to development, production, and abandonment decisions. It least distorts the time distribution of production, and it most rewards operators for efficiency. Royalty bidding, in contrast, causes less capacity to be installed and encourages premature abandonment. Profit-share bidding reduces the reward for cost-saving and efficiency. The system of leasing most conducive to conservation is thus bonus bidding.

Unfortunately, bonus bidding alone is not enough to ensure conservation of oil and gas. It is well known that where there are two or more operators in a common reservoir, there is an externality in a given operator's incentives to produce. The faster a given operator produces, the more oil or gas he drains from his neighbor's land. Each operator is therefore motivated to install too much capacity and to produce too rapidly vis-à-vis considerations of conservation. Not only is the time distribution of production distorted toward the present, but in the case of oil, ultimate recovery is reduced. This is the major conservation problem in oil and gas production, and almost everywhere it has given rise to some form of production regulation.

On the OCS, oil and gas production is regulated by the U.S. Geological Survey, an agency also associated with the leasing and enforcement process. The primary tool of production regulation on the OCS is the concept of the "maximum efficient rate" of production (MER), defined as that rate of production which if exceeded will result in significant loss of ultimate recovery. Operators are not permitted to produce at a rate faster than MER because conservation is viewed as prevention of physical waste (such as loss of ultimate recovery). Operators are motivated to produce at no lower rate, for if one operator does so, he invites drainage to the lands of operators who do not. So, in effect MER becomes the minimum as well as the maximum rate of production—and capacity is installed consistent with that rate. It is clear that if conservation calls for changes in the production rate when interest rates and relative prices change, MER-based regulation does not satisfy the requirements of conservation. It is further clear that prevention of loss of ultimate recovery at whatever cost in terms of present value is a simplistic, naive notion of conservation.

The obvious solution is not to regulate production but to remove the externality that causes the conservation problem when production is unregulated. This can be done simply by requiring unitization of all reservoirs in which there are two or more competing operators.[4] Since unitized operators share by contract in all revenues and costs, there is no motivation for one operator to try to secure oil or gas at the expense of his neighbor. Given freedom, the unit manager will seek to maximize present value of the reservoir as a whole (and therefore of each lease), and he will respond appropriately to changes in interest rates and relative prices. Conservation will result from profit motivation of the unit manager and those whom he represents. In the case of single-operator reservoirs, unitization automatically exists, and freedom for the operator is all that is required.

Why be concerned with this in a study of leasing procedures? There is a sense, of course, in which conservation regulation and leasing practice are separate problems. There is a more fundamental sense in which they cannot be separated. The proper aim of government as lessor is to maximize the present value of rent receipts. To do this, the present value of the resource must be maximized. There must be conservation, including intertemporal efficiency, if the government is to capture all the rent that is there. This can only result, under private exploitation of the resource, if reservoirs are systematically unitized so that prospective lessees can anticipate the results of unitization in their calculations of present value. Clearly, if operators can anticipate maximization of present value, they will bid more for a lease than if they can only anticipate regulation, such as that based on MER, which practically assures diminished present value.

Many reservoirs on the OCS have only one lessee-operator. Many more have only a few, and often those are already associated in connection with joint bids. Most OCS operators are sophisticated and appreciate the benefits of unitization from their own private point of view. Unitization is relatively simple on the OCS in contrast to the mainland, where there are often many landowners over a reservoir as well as multiple operators. The Secretary of the Interior has the statutory power to compel unitization and to prescribe a unit plan of operation where that is necessary to achieve prompt unitization. There is thus no reason why unitization, combined with operator freedom as to well density and production rates, should not become the rule on the OCS as a measure of conservation and therefore

---

4. Unitization consists of pooling separate leases for the limited purpose of operating a reservoir as a single unit, selecting a unit manager, and agreeing on a formula for sharing costs and revenues. A plan of operation may also be a part of the contract.

an instrument of securing the maximum present value of rent for the government as landowner. Bonus leasing, with its connotations of efficiency, combines well with unitization and operator freedom.

There remains the problem of environmental protection. Like conservation, environmental protection is a matter of an externality, except that the externality is a social cost not necessarily borne by the industry causing it. Without environmental protection, oil and gas operators perceive prospects as promising more net cash flow than otherwise, and they pay too much to the government for the privilege of exploration, development, and production. In effect, a part of the "rent" payments to the government is a tax on environmental amenities. Too much "rent" is just as harmful to society as too little. The appropriate goal is to capture all the true rent, no more and no less.

As with conservation, the solution is to internalize the externality and otherwise give operators freedom to maximize profits. The cost of environmental damage should be borne in the first instance by operators so that their marginal costs will reflect all social costs and the margin between domestic production and imports will be economically appropriate. For example, if operators know in advance that they will be required to clean up oil spills and compensate injured parties, they will be motivated to take cost-effective steps to minimize such spills (incurring expense, of course) and they will embody this and other prospective expenses (such as oil spill insurance, which is available to small firms that cannot self-insure) in estimates of future cash flow. Government will receive less "rent" but that received will be true rent and not a tax on amenities. Thus, although environmental protection is in a sense a matter distinct from leasing practice, it is highly relevant to the goal of capturing all rent, no more and no less.

One could go on and on with this foreword, giving additional foretastes of what is to come in this excellent book. But it is time to turn to the real thing. The reader can look forward to ample reward.

— **Stephen L. McDonald**
University of Texas, Austin

ACKNOWLEDGMENTS

Our research of federal policies governing Outer Continental Shelf oil and gas leases began over two decades ago. Over the last six years this research has been funded in part by the U.S. Geological Survey (USGS) (1978–1981) and by the Pacific Institute for Public Policy Research (1984). The former support allowed us to develop a data base and ultimately resulted in the writing of several technical reports for the government as well as doctoral theses, journal articles, and several papers presented at professional conferences. The latter support should be credited with the writing of this volume.

In the process of our research we have become indebted to a number of persons and organizations. We would like to acknowledge the generous assistance provided by numerous individuals employed in the oil industry who helped us to acquire necessary data relating to offshore exploration and development, and taxation of income derived from OCS activities. We also thank the federal and state government officials who assisted us in developing our data base, particularly the staff of USGS Conservation Division Offices in Reston, Virginia, and Metairie, Louisiana. In particular, we acknowledge the years of patient and constructive collaboration in our early research of Government Technical Officers John Lohrenz, Holly Tomlinson, and John Bratland. We extend our special thanks to Dr. Russell O. Jones for his important contributions to our empirical analysis in its early stages.

Our research benefited greatly from its exposure to the profession. Of the many academic economists who commented on our work in its early stages, we owe special thanks to Dr. Stephen L. McDonald of the University of Texas, Austin, and to Dr. James L. Smith of the University of Illinois.

We also thank the Community and Organization Research Institute of the University of California at Santa Barbara, under whose auspices the various grants supporting our research were administered and many of our manuscripts typed, and California State University, Long Beach, for allowing the release time necessary for Dr. Muraoka to contribute to this work.

It goes without saying that none of the individuals who helped us in the development of our research is responsible for any remaining errors. The conclusions reported here are those of the authors and are not necessarily endorsed by any of the individuals or organizations mentioned above.

This book is dedicated to four extraordinary people, with thanks for their limitless patience and encouragement: Thelma Mead, Corine Klingbeil, Mimi Muraoka, and Joyce Sorensen.

Walter J. Mead
University of California at Santa Barbara
Asbjorn Moseidjord
St. Mary's College of California
Dennis D. Muraoka
California State University, Long Beach
Philip E. Sorensen
Florida State University

INTRODUCTION

This is a book about the public management of a national treasure, the minerals that underlie the Outer Continental Shelf. Most experts agree that the greater part of the undiscovered domestic reserves of crude oil and natural gas lie in the public domain offshore. Federal and state governments are also the trustees for lands that contain vast quantities of other mineral resources including coal and oil shale, and renewable resources including the national forests.

In general, the government has chosen not to develop these resources itself but has sold development rights to the private sector. The policy of transferring resource rights to private parties has always been controversial. Some of the greatest political scandals in U.S. history, such as Teapot Dome, have grown out of questionable transfers of rights to public resources. For this reason, the government seldom relinquishes full control over public resources to private firms. In the modern era, there have been three major arguments favoring the policy of maintaining some control over resource development: (1) to protect the government's share of resource value, (2) to ensure that the environment is protected, and (3) to protect the interests of future generations. The intentional control that the government maintains is indicative that public administrators, politicians, and the public at large still do not trust private sector control over publicly owned resources. In particular, legislation enacted during the 1970s expressed increasing distrust of the ability of the private sector to manage offshore mineral resources properly. One of the main objectives of this study is to determine whether this mistrust is warranted.

Our philosophical approach to resource management analysis is founded on classical microeconomic principles. These principles hold that competitive markets (under certain attainable conditions) correctly determine resource and product prices and efficiently allocate scarce resources between present and future generations. Economic theory suggests that the government as the trustee of natural resources should manage them in a way that maximizes what economists call "economic rent." Economic rent is the difference between the market value of the resource and all of the necessary costs of its production. Using this economic framework, it can be shown that if the trustee government selects resource management policies that create incentives counter to efficient production or impose wasteful procedures on the private lease operator, the cost of these policies is paid out of economic rent and is borne by the public in the form of reduced living standards. The goal of resource conservation is not served. Thus, resource management policies chosen by the government may either serve or undermine the goal of conservation and the public interest.

The research serving as the foundation for this book was conducted at the University of California at Santa Barbara over a period of nearly two decades. At the same time, closely related research investigated the sale of cutting rights to federal timber by the U.S. Forest Service (USFS) in the Pacific Northwest. The competitive issues and policy problems of selling public timber are similar to those of selling oil and gas leases. These research efforts were funded by the federal government—the U.S. Geological Survey in the Department of the Interior, and the USFS in the Department of Agriculture. Reports were issued to these agencies as various phases of the work were completed. In this volume we have synthesized much of this research, with particular emphasis on the management of the Outer Continental Shelf (OCS).

Chapter 1 reviews the legal framework of OCS leasing and traces the history of offshore leasing from the first state of Louisiana offshore leases in the 1940s to the present. This chapter also addresses the main pieces of legislation governing federal offshore leasing—in particular, the OCS Lands Act of 1953 as amended in 1978. Chapter 2 builds the economic foundation for an analysis of offshore leasing. It provides a detailed description of the concept of economic rent. The economic meaning of conservation is also presented and is contrasted with other widely held definitions of conservation. In its economic conception, conservation addresses the allocation of resources both within a given time period and across all time periods. Those readers with a background in economics will immediately recognize that the economic definition of conservation is synonymous with economic efficiency. Chapter 2 also considers the nature of a market allocation of resources and analyzes the question of whether a market allocation is consistent with resource conservation.

Chapters 3 and 4 address the economic implications of alternative leasing methods. Chapter 3 contains a theoretical and empirical investigation of the traditional method of issuing federal OCS leases, cash bonus bidding with a fixed royalty. This method of leasing has been criticized for restricting competition and failing to return the fair market value of public lease rights to the government. Results of our empirical analyses of the traditional bonus bid leasing system are reported, based on 1,223 federal Gulf of Mexico leases issued from 1954 through 1969, with a record of oil and gas production extending through 1979. This empirical research was designed to answer the questions raised by critics of bonus bid leasing: Are the results the outcome of competitive market processes? Did the government get fair value for its lease rights? Chapter 4 considers the alternative methods of payment for offshore leases that have been authorized by the federal government. In particular, it examines the effects of royalty, profit share, and work commitment leasing from the perspective of resource conservation. This chapter is primarily theoretical because there has been little experience in the United States using these leasing methods. Nevertheless, the limited empirical evidence of the effects of these payment methods is presented.

Chapter 5 focuses on additional issues in offshore leasing. In particular we define the economic meaning of "expeditious development" and investigate whether lessees have developed their offshore properties diligently. Next the auction method employed at OCS lease sales is examined to determine whether oral or sealed bidding yields superior results. This is followed by a study of the optimal size of an offshore lease tract. In particular we ask, Are offshore lease tracts too large or too small? Next the minimum bid and bid rejection procedures for offshore leases are discussed, with particular attention to the necessity for these procedures. Finally we turn our attention to the political opposition to offshore leasing. Specifically, we seek to explain the resistance to OCS leasing by state and local governments and by environmental organizations.

Chapter 6 summarizes our results and presents our recommendations for offshore leasing policy. Many of our recommendations for OCS leasing policy apply with equal force to state oil and gas leasing and to the sale or lease of other natural resources. Given the controversy that continues to surround the management of publicly owned resources generally, it is our hope that this research will add substance to the debate in this important area and, most important, help to forge improved policies to conserve the natural resources of our nation.

1

THE HISTORICAL AND LEGAL FRAMEWORK OF OUTER CONTINENTAL SHELF LEASING

In this chapter we examine the historical and legal framework of Outer Continental Shelf (OCS) leasing. The chapter begins with a brief discussion of OCS leasing, including some pertinent definitions. This is followed by a discussion of the history of offshore leasing, which began with leases issued by the state of Louisana in the 1940s and 1950s. We then present the legal framework of federal offshore leasing, including an analysis of the main pieces of legislation in this area from the OCS Lands Act of 1953 to the OCS Lands Act Amendments of 1978.

AN INTRODUCTION TO OFFSHORE LEASING

Offshore oil was first produced from a pier located in state waters at Summerland, California (near Santa Barbara), in 1897. During the ensuing decades, techniques for production from deeper waters have rapidly developed and have pushed the frontier of drilling activity from inland marshes and lakes to coastal bays and, finally, into the waters of the Outer Continental Shelf.

The continental shelf is the shallow, gently sloping portion of the continental margin that extends from the coastline to the more steeply inclined continental slope, as shown in Figure 1-1. These lands are within the public domain and come under the jurisdiction of either federal or state governments. The first three miles from the shoreline are under the

Figure 1–1. The Continental Margin in Profile (Average Water Depths in Meters).

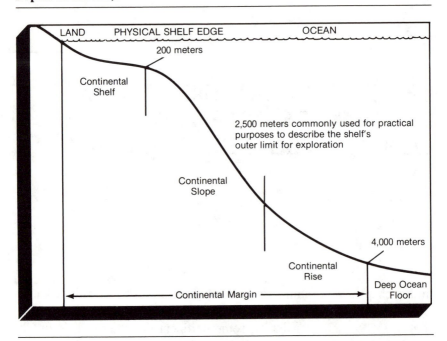

SOURCE: Adapted from U.S. General Accounting Office, Comptroller General's Report to Congress, *Issues in Leasing Offshore Lands for Oil and Gas Development*, EMD-81-59, 26 March 1981, p. 2; and U.S. Department of the Interior, *Energy Resources on Federally Administered Land*, 1981.

jurisdiction of the adjacent state governments, with the exception of the lands adjacent to Texas and the west coast of Florida, where the first 10.4 miles (three marine leagues) are under state jurisdiction. The United States Supreme Court ruled that these states were entitled to the wider boundary because they had held those lands as sovereign nations at the time of their admission to the Union. Lands lying beyond the state waters and out to a distance of 200 miles from shore come under the jurisdiction of the federal government. These lands are known as the Outer Continental Shelf, or OCS. Given the present technical capacity for underwater drilling and production, the economically valuable areas of the OCS are at water depths shallower than 8,200 feet (2,500 meters). The total area of the OCS to this depth, shown in Figure 1–2, is approximately 819.2

Figure 1–2. Outer Continental Shelf Areas Under Leasing Consideration (Shown at 200 Meter and 2500 Meter Water Depths).

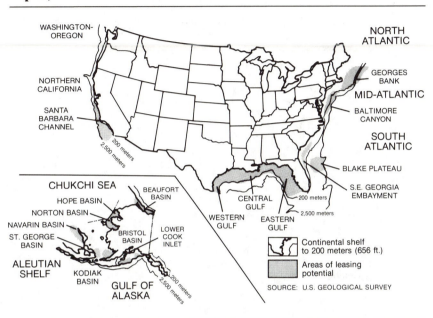

Source: U.S. General Accounting Office, Comptroller General's Report to Congress, *Issues in Leasing Offshore Lands for Oil and Gas Development*, EMD-81-59, 26 March 1981, p. 2.

million acres—an area equal to 36 percent of the total land area of the United States.[1]

OCS lands lie in four regions—Alaska, the Atlantic, the Gulf of Mexico, and the Pacific. Government estimates of OCS acreage within these regions are displayed in Figure 1–3, which shows that over half of these submerged lands lie offshore Alaska. In addition to these lands, 32.7 million offshore acres come under state jurisdiction.

Through August 1983, 29.8 million acres have been leased for oil and gas development in eighty OCS lease sales, in which 6,005 oil and gas

1. The true acreage cannot be known with exact precision, but estimates range from the figure cited above to 1,150 million acres. See Comptroller General's Report to Congress, *Issues in Leasing Offshore Lands for Oil and Gas Development*, EMD-81-59 (Washington, D.C.: General Accounting Office, 1981), p. 3.

Figure 1–3. Outer Continental Shelf Acreage by Region (Millions of Acres[a]/Water Depth).

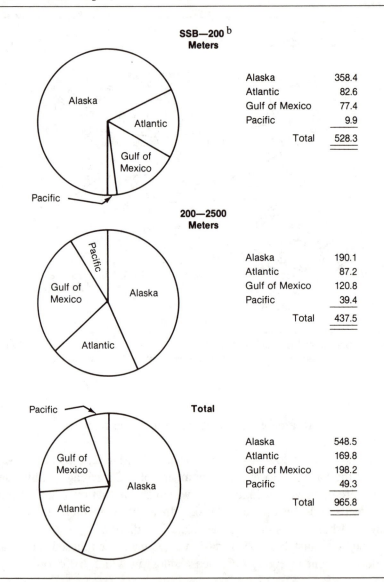

SSB—200 [b]
Meters

Alaska	358.4
Atlantic	82.6
Gulf of Mexico	77.4
Pacific	9.9
Total	528.3

200—2500
Meters

Alaska	190.1
Atlantic	87.2
Gulf of Mexico	120.8
Pacific	39.4
Total	437.5

Total

Alaska	548.5
Atlantic	169.8
Gulf of Mexico	198.2
Pacific	49.3
Total	965.8

SOURCE: Comptroller General's Report to Congress, *Issues in Leasing Offshore Lands for Oil and Gas Development*, EMD-81-59, 26 March 1981, p. 4.

[a]Reflects GAO's consolidation of offshore land area data provided by the Department of the Interior and Exxon Company, U.S.A. Does not include Hawaii's approximate 4 million acres of OCS.
[b]SSB = States Seaward Boundaries

leases were issued.[2] This acreage is approximately 3 to 4 percent of total OCS acreage. Substantial quantities of crude oil and natural gas have been located in the Gulf of Mexico (particularly offshore from Louisiana and Texas), offshore California, and offshore Alaska. The annual production figures from federal OCS lands are shown in Table 1-1.

Through 1982, OCS oil and gas leases have produced $105.5 billion in gross revenue and $58.9 billion in bonus, royalty, and rental payments to the federal government.[3] The U.S. Geological Survey has estimated that 16.9 to 43.5 billion barrels of oil and 117.4 to 230.6 trillion cubic feet of natural gas lie undiscovered offshore.[4] This accounts for 40.5 to 61.3 percent of the estimated undiscovered natural gas in the United States.[5]

THE FIRST OFFSHORE LEASES

The initial government leasing of OCS lands was not undertaken by the federal government but by the state of Louisiana. Sensing the economic potential of its offshore oil and gas lands, Louisiana created a State Mineral Board in 1936. The board was directed to select acreage for leasing, grant leases based on competitive auctions, and collect revenue from offshore production. In the absence of any legal precedent giving the federal government title to OCS lands, Louisiana and other coastal states invited nominations for, and then proceeded to lease, large areas of the OCS in the post–World War II period. By 1950, Louisiana and Texas had leased almost 5 million acres of offshore lands for oil and gas development.

The leasing policy adopted by Louisiana (which is still in use today in that state) permitted two bid variables to be specified for each lease: (1) a cash bonus, and (2) a royalty rate. A bonus is a lump-sum cash payment made at the time the lease is granted. If no oil or gas is found, the lease expires after five to ten years. In this event, the nonrefundable bonus payment is kept by the government and the lessee's losses are the sum of his bonus payment, his small annual rental payments, and his investment in exploration and drilling. If, on the other hand, reserves are discovered, they become the property of the lessee, with no further bonus payment required. A royalty is a contingency payment required of lessees only if

2. U.S. Department of the Interior, Mineral Management Service, *Federal Offshore Statistics,* Dec. 1983, pp. 8–11.

3. Ibid., pp. 40–41.

4. U.S. Geological Survey, *Geological Estimates of Undiscovered Recoverable Conventional Resources of Oil and Gas in the United States, A Summary,* Circular 860, 1981.

5. Ibid.

Table 1–1. Annual Crude Oil and Natural Gas Production From the Federal OCS, 1954–1982.

Year	Crude Oil and Condensate (million barrels)	Natural Gas (billion cubic feet)
Prior	1.2	19.9
1954	3.3	56.3
1955	6.7	81.3
1956	11.0	82.9
1957	16.1	82.6
1958	24.8	127.7
1959	35.7	207.2
1960	49.7	273.0
1961	64.3	318.3
1962	89.7	452.0
1963	104.6	564.4
1964	122.5	621.7
1965	145.0	645.6
1966	188.7	1,007.4
1967	221.9	1,187.2
1968	269.9	1,524.2
1969	312.9	1,954.5
1970	360.6	2,418.7
1971	418.5	2,777.0
1972	411.9	3,038.6
1973	394.7	3,211.6
1974	360.6	3,514.7
1975	330.2	3,458.7
1976	316.9	3,595.9
1977	303.9	3,737.7
1978	292.3	4,385.1
1979	285.6	4,673.0
1980	277.4	4,641.5
1981	286.6	4,844.5
1982	321.2	4,679.5
Total[*]	6,027.4	58,182.5

Source: U.S. Department of the Interior, Mineral Management Service, *Federal Offshore Statistics*, Dec. 1983, pp. 44–45.

[*]Total may not add up due to rounding error.

oil or gas is discovered and production ensues. It is a percentage of the total production from the lease.

In the initial Louisiana leases, the royalty rate (subject to a statutory 12.5 percent minimum) and the bonus payment were both determined by competitive bidding. For any lease offered, the highest bid on both these variables would determine the winner. In the event that no single bid was highest with respect to both bid variables, the State Mineral Board was empowered to accept the higher royalty bid in combination with a smaller bonus bid (or vice versa), at its discretion.

The claims by Louisiana and other coastal states to offshore resources were highly controversial. State claims were based on debatable interpretations of common law, implied grants of power to the states by the Constitution, and the absence of any direct claims to these resources by the federal government. In an Executive Order dated September 28, 1945, President Truman preempted any possible claims to jurisdiction over these resources by other nations, declaring that "the natural resources of the subsoil and seabed of the continental shelf . . . contiguous to the coasts of the United States are declared this day by proclamation to appertain to the United States and be subject to its jurisdiction and control. . . ."

The legal position of the coastal states with respect to offshore resources was settled in the Tidelands Cases of 1947–50. The fundamental findings of the Supreme Court, first expressed in *United States v. California* (June 23, 1947), were as follows:

> The United States is now, and has been at all times pertinent hereto, possessed of paramount rights in, and full dominion and power over, the lands, minerals and other things underlying the Pacific Ocean lying seaward of the ordinary low water mark on the coast of California. . . . The State of California has no title thereto or property interest therein.

Later declarations by the Supreme Court held that Louisiana and Texas stood on no better footing than did California. Since these states had already leased lands in the area affected by the decision and were receiving royalties from those lands, a full accounting of revenue derived from the area had to be made, with these funds returned to the federal government.

With the rights of the coastal states to any claims upon the offshore resources effectively foreclosed, Congress was pressed to enact legislation that would divide offshore lands between state and federal jurisdictions. This was acomplished in the Submerged Lands Act of 1953, which assigned to the states all title to offshore lands lying within three miles of the coast (except for Texas and Florida, as noted earlier).[6]

A major complication, which was not resolved in drawing the state-federal offshore boundary, was the status of leases issued by Louisiana and Texas prior to the decisions in the Tidelands cases. Legal authorities agreed that the leases were null and void. However, the Senate Committee on Interior and Insular Affairs was shown figures indicating that more than $234 million had been spent by oil companies in "good faith" lease bonuses and other investments as of July 15, 1950. The committee was also told,

> The returns from operations thus far conducted on the Continental Shelf area are too meager to offer any real inducement for these operators to continue to operate and to spend their money in drilling new wells and in exploration unless they have some definite assurance that these leases will be confirmed so...a complete and clear-cut confirmation of these leases is essential in order to obtain this continued development.[7]

THE OCS LANDS ACT OF 1953

Congress responded to the problem of the previously issued leases (also referred to as Section 6 leases) in the OCS Lands Act of 1953 (Public Law 83-212).[8] Contracts with the original lessees were honored by the federal government, and administration of the leases was transferred to the U.S. Geological Survey (USGS), a division of the Department of the Interior. Congress further required a full accounting of all revenues received by Louisiana and Texas from such leases, and instituted a new requirement in all leases that a minimum royalty of 12.5 percent would apply to all production, regardless of the original terms to the state leases.[9]

The 1953 act authorized the Secretary of the Department of the Interior to select acreage on the OCS to be leased to private parties, offer such acreage for lease through competitive bidding, and administer the leases according to the rules laid down in the act. It also authorized the Secretary to issue more detailed rules—as needed to satisfy the provisions of the act—governing the exploration, development, production, and transportation activities of the OCS oil and gas industry.

6. 43 U.S.C. 1301–1315.

7. Statement by Hines H. Baker, President, Humble Oil Company, *Hearings Before the Committee on Interior and Insular Affairs,* U.S. Senate, 81st Congress, 2nd session, August 14–19, 1950, p. 86.

8. 43 U.S.C. 1331–1343.

9. The practical effect of the last requirement was small for the Louisiana Section 6 leases because all but seven of the 271 leases issued were bid at a 12.5 percent royalty.

Within the Department of the Interior, the Bureau of Land Management (BLM) and the USGS have primary responsibility for leasing OCS lands. The leasing process generally starts with the BLM making a resource evaluation of a broad area and issuing a report. Thereafter, an invitation to nominate specific tracts within this area is published in the *Federal Register*. A preliminary tract selection is then made, based on industry interest as indicated in the tract nominations together with tracts recommended by the USGS and by the BLM itself. Selected tracts cannot exceed 5,760 acres.[10] Environmental impact statements are then initiated by the BLM in accordance with the National Environmental Policy Act of 1969.[11] Since 1968, the USGS has made tract-specific geologic, engineering, and economic evaluations. An important objective of these evaluations has been to estimate the economic value of each tract at the time of the auction. The input data for the computerized simulations used by the USGS are data submitted by lessees of nearby tracts. The estimated tract values have been used in conjunction with other criteria to decide whether to accept the high bids submitted at the auction. These values are not made public until after the sale.

At least ninety days in advance of the sale, information on the location of possible tracts to be offered is made available—by means of a draft environmental impact statement—to potential bidders, environmental groups, state and local governments, and other interested parties. Following public hearings, a final environmental impact statement is prepared and submitted to the President's Council on Environmental Quality. The Secretary of the Interior makes the final decision as to whether or not to hold a sale and as to what environmental restrictions are to be included in the sale terms. These terms are made public in the notice of final tract selection, which is published at least thirty days prior to the sale. This information allows potential bidders to carry out tract-specific exploratory activity in order to develop a bidding strategy.

The notice of final tract selection includes a specification of what bidding system is to be used. The OCS Lands Act of 1953 specified that OCS lands must be leased through competitive bidding, using sealed bid auctions. The bidding variables were specified to be a cash bonus with fixed royalty of not less than 12.5 percent, or a royalty bid of at least 12.5 percent together with a fixed bonus payment.[12] The Secretary of the Interior

10. 43 U.S.C. 1337(b).
11. 42 U.S.C. 4321–4347.
12. 43 U.S.C. 1337(a).

was granted the authority to determine which of these two systems would be employed. Before 1978, the Interior Department employed, with few exceptions, the cash bonus leasing system with a fixed royalty rate of 16⅔ percent (one-sixth) of the value of production.[13] The Secretary was also authorized to collect annual rental payments from lessees on all non-producing leases.[14] The primary term of the lease was normally five years, although some more recent leases in frontier areas have carried a ten-year term. The longer lease terms have been used when water depths exceed 900 meters, and in very high cost areas such as Alaska. The lessee can retain the lease beyond this period, however, as long as the lease is producing in paying quantities or, upon approval of the Secretary, as long as drilling or reworking operations are taking place.[15]

Bidders may submit either a solo or a joint bid. The National Energy Policy and Conservation Act of 1975 (PL 94-163) has restricted joint bidding among oil companies whose worldwide production is greater than 1.6 million barrels per day. No more than one of these companies can participate in any given joint bid. (Exceptions to this rule have been made for high-risk frontier areas.) Nine companies have been affected by this restriction: Arco, Sohio-British Petroleum, Exxon, Gulf, Mobil, Shell, Standard Oil of California, Standard Oil of Indiana, and Texaco.

The BLM, which administers the bid auction, has the right to reject any bid that is submitted by an unqualified bidder, thought to be fraudulent, or thought not to reflect the tract value adequately. A winning bidder obtains the exclusive right to explore for, develop, and produce from petroleum deposits located on the specified tract. He may sell this right subject to approval from the Secretary of the Interior or he may "farm the lease out" to other companies. Throughout the life of the lease, the BLM and USGS share responsibility for ensuring that lessees adhere to the terms of the lease, as well as the other rules that govern the OCS industry.

THE ENVIRONMENTAL LEGISLATION— 1969 THROUGH 1977

From 1953 through 1963, federal offshore leasing was limited to the Gulf of Mexico. Federal leasing of the Pacific OCS commenced in 1963, and

13. Of the 3,162 leases issued by the federal government from 1954 through 1977, 3,124 (98.8 percent) were issued using cash bonus bidding with a fixed royalty and thirty-eight (1.2 percent) were issued using royalty bidding with a fixed bonus.

14. 43 U.S.C. 1337(b).

15. 43 U.S.C. 1337(b).

in 1966 the first federal leases in the Santa Barbara Channel, off Southern California, were issued. In February 1968, the federal government conducted an auction covering the Dos Cuadras oil field in the Santa Barbara Channel. (These particular leases were later to draw unprecedented national attention.) Tract 402 in the Dos Cuadras field was awarded to Union Oil Company and its partners—Gulf, Mobil, and Texaco—for $61.4 million. Shortly thereafter, Platform A was set into place. On January 28, 1969, the fifth well drilled from the platform blew out. After eleven days, on February 8, 1969, the well was finally plugged but not before thousands of barrels of oil had spilled into the channel and ultimately onto the nearby beaches.[16] The resulting damage to sea birds, fish, and the marine environment generally was graphically documented in local and national news reports showing dying seagulls and the carcass of a sea lion in a pool of oily muck. In fact, the total social cost of the Santa Barbara oil spill was about $16.4 million (1969 dollars).[17] But the impact of the oil spill was far more dramatic. It is now widely accepted that the Santa Barbara oil spill was the catalyst that led Congress to pass stringent environmental and pollution regulations, including the National Environmental Policy Act of 1969, the Marine Sanctuaries Act of 1972, the Coastal Zone Management Act of 1972, the Endangered Species Act of 1973, and the Clean Water Act as amended in 1977. The impact of these statutes on OCS oil and gas development is summarized in a report to Congress by the Comptroller General of the United States.

> This legislation, among other things, (1) emphasized the prevention and elimination of damage to the environment; (2) called for the preservation and/or protection of the natural habitat and its inhabitants; and (3) encouraged the participation of the public, other OCS users, and the coastal States in managing coastal zones. These laws brought many Federal and State agencies into managing OCS activities and required regulations and administrative procedures—complete with forms and reports—to clarify statutory intent and achieve statutory goals.[18]

16. The President's Panel on Oil Spills reviewed several estimates of spill volume and concluded that the total spillage was between 1 and 3 million gallons (24,000 to 71,000 barrels).

17. Walter J. Mead and Philip E. Sorensen, "The Economic Cost of the Santa Barbara Oil Spill," in *Santa Barbara Oil Spill: An Environmental Inquiry,* University of California at Santa Barbara, California Marine Science Institute, Santa Barbara, California, 1972.

18. U.S. General Accounting Office, Comptroller General's Report to Congress, *Impact of Regulations—After Federal Leasing—on Outer Continental Shelf Oil and Gas Development,* EMD-81-48, 27 Feb. 1981, p. 2.

THE OCS LANDS ACT AMENDMENTS OF 1978

The OCS Lands Act Amendments of 1978 (Public Law 95-372) reflect the rising power of several political interest groups and the dissatisfaction of Congress with the Interior Department's administration of the 1953 act.[19] Analysis of the 1978 amendments reveals four general areas of criticism of the 1953 act.

The first, expressed by consumer activists (including a lobbying group called Energy Action), asserted that the primary leasing system in use, cash bonus bidding with a one-sixth royalty, had not produced competitive results, that the government had not received "fair market value" for its leases, and that big oil companies enjoyed an unfair advantage in the lease-sale market.[20] A second body of opinion, representing environmental groups and land use planners, wanted the federal government to expand its planning role in OCS development. The third group consisted of coastal state politicians, state-level planners, and environmental regulators who argued that they should be given increased powers concerning the location, timing, and scope of offshore activities conducted near their coastlines. Finally, governors of coastal states and private groups, whose interests conflicted with offshore energy development, wanted financial protection against the risk of losses that they might bear as a result of offshore mineral leasing. The 1953 legislation gave no share of OCS revenues to coastal states, but the latter were nevertheless expected to accept the risk of economic and environmental damage resulting from OCS development.

The provisions of the 1978 amendments show a fundamental distrust of the ability of markets to allocate and manage OCS resources properly, as evidenced by the comprehensive regulatory and planning powers granted to various federal and state administrative agencies. The principal changes are outlined below.

1. Whereas the 1953 act authorized only cash bonus or royalty bidding, the amendments specify eight alternative bidding systems and authorize any combination of these bidding arrangements, plus any

---

19. This section is based on R. O. Jones, W. J. Mead, and P. E. Sorensen, "The Outer Continental Shelf Lands Act Amendments of 1978," *Natural Resources Journal* 19 (Oct. 1979): 885–908.

20. In his endorsement of the proposed amendments, President Carter asserted that they would "enhance competition [and] ensure a fair return to the public." See Executive Office of the President, The National Energy Plan 56 (1977).

other system that might occur to the Secretary of the Interior.[21] The task of implementing the alternative leasing systems was initially shared by the Department of the Interior and the Department of Energy (DOE). Developing regulations for the experimental bidding systems was assigned to the DOE. While the Interior Department was given the responsibility of selecting a leasing system for a particular sale, DOE had the authority to review Interior's selection and to disapprove selections that it deemed inappropriate. Table 1–2 describes the systems promulgated by DOE.[22]

The leasing systems permitted under the 1978 amendments include the two allowed under the OCS Lands Act of 1953 plus four new systems with two new bid variables: net profit-share and work commitment.[23]

Congress specified that bidding systems other than the conventional cash bonus bid with a fixed royalty must be used for between 20 and 60 percent of the total area offered for leasing each year during the first five years following enactment of the legislation.[24] In addition, the Interior Secretary was authorized to defer payment for up to five years on any part of a cash bonus, whether the bonus was a bid variable or a fixed factor.[25]

An unusual provision of the new legislation authorized the Secretary to allow multiple bidding on the same tract using any two or more of the alternatives listed in Table 1–2 on no more than 10 percent of the tracts offered each year.[26] The Secretary was also autho-

---

21. 43 U.S.C.A. 1337 (a) (1) (Supp. 1979).

22. The Department of Interior Appropriations Act for fiscal year 1982 (Public Law 97-100) repealed DOE responsibilities in implementing the alternative systems and assigned them to the Interior Department.

23. Work commitment bidding awards the lease to the firm that pledges to undertake the greatest dollar amount of exploration on the lease. An important difference between the U.S. and the North Sea work commitment bidding systems is that in the former, there is only one bid variable, while in the latter, there are several bid variables—and potential bidders may not always know what they are. Only the U.S. version is considered here. For more detail on the North Sea system, see K. W. Dam, *Oil Resources* (Chicago: University of Chicago Press, 1976). In the U.S. system, the lessee is required to remit the cash value of the bid, or a performance bond for the same amount, at the time the lease is issued. During the exploration phase and as long as cumulative exploration costs are less than the work commitment bid, the lessee is refunded one-half of the exploration costs. The lessee may terminate exploration at any time, and thus the U.S. system does not obligate the lessee to satisfy his work commitment bid.

24. 43 U.S.C.A. 1337 (a)(5)(B).

25. Id. 1337(a)(2).

26. Id. 1337(a)(5)(A).

Table 1–2. Alternative Leasing Systems for Outer Continental Shelf Oil and Gas Prospects.

Leasing System	Public Notice[a]	Bid Variable	Public Revenue Collected by Means of[b]			
			Cash Bonus	Royalty	Annual Rental	Net Profit-Share
(1) Cash Bonus Bidding with Fixed Royalty Rate	02-12-80	Cash bonus, payable at lease sale date	*	* (minimum 12½%)	*	
(2) Cash Bonus Bidding with Sliding Scale Royalty Rate	02-12-80	Cash bonus, payable at lease sale date	*	* (minimum 12½%)	*	
(3) Cash Bonus Bidding with Fixed Net Profit-Share	05-30-80	Cash bonus, payable at lease sale date	*		*	* (minimum 30%)
(4) Royalty Rate Bidding	02-12-80	Royalty as a percentage at production value or quantity	*	*	*	
(5) Work Commitment Bidding	07-09-81	Dollar value of exploration program	*	*	*	
(6) Net Profit-Share Bidding	06-02-81	Percentage of net profits	*		*	*

Source: Derived from W. J. Mead, A. Moseidjord, and D. D. Muraoka, "Alternative Bid Variables as Instruments of OCS Leasing Policy," *Contemporary Policy Issues* 1 (no. 5, March 1984):32.

[a] The public notice specifying applicable rules and regulations appeared in the Federal Register at the indicated dates.

[b] The means for collecting revenue other than the bid variable are determined by discretion of the Secretary of the Department of the Interior and published in the lease sale notice. They may vary from tract to tract, but are subject to the limits indicated in the table. Under the work commitment bidding system, the public also receives the maximum of (1) one-half the amount bid and (2) the difference between the amount bid and one-half the actual exploration costs.

rized to award leases using bidding alternatives selected at random.[27] In the language of the act, the purpose of this section was "to obtain statistical information to determine which bidding alternative will best accomplish the purposes and policies of the Act."[28] Table 1-3 summarizes the use of these leasing systems over the period 1979–1982.[29]

2. The 1978 legislation mandated a significant expansion in economic planning. The Interior Secretary was required to set forth a five-year leasing plan with annual revisions.[30] The plan was to consist of a schedule of proposed lease sales incorporating management of the

Table 1-3. Leasing Systems Used in Outer Continental Shelf Oil and Gas Lease Sales, 1979-1982.

Year	Number of Leases Issued	Cash Bonus With a Fixed Royalty Rate[a]		Cash Bonus With a Sliding Scale Royalty Rate		Cash Bonus With Fixed Net Profit-Share	
		No.	*%*	*No.*	*%*	*No.*	*%*
1979	351	176	50.1	175	49.9	0	0
1980	218	118	54.1	41	18.8	59	27.1
1981	369	255	69.1	0	0	114	30.9
1982	358	316	88.3	25	7.0	17	4.7

SOURCE: Derived from W. J. Mead, A. Moseidjord, and D. D. Muraoka, "Alternative Bid Variables as Instruments of OCS Leasing Policy," *Contemporary Policy Issues* 1 (no. 5, March 1984): 33. Prior to 1979, nearly all leases were issued on the basis of cash bonus bidding, with a royalty rate of 16⅔ percent.

U.S. Department of the Interior, Bureau of Land Management, *Outer Continental Shelf Statistical Summary, 1979-1981.*

U.S. General Accounting Office, Comptroller General's Report to Congress, *Congress Should Extend Mandate to Experiment With Alternative Bidding Systems in Leasing Offshore Lands,* GAO/RCED-83-139, 27 May 1983.

[a] Includes leases with royalty rates at 12½%, 16⅔%, and 33⅓%.

27. Id.
28. Id.
29. In a suit brought by Energy Action against the Department of the Interior it was alleged that these provisions of the 1978 amendments were not being met because all of the leasing methods described by the amendments had not been used. In fact, while the fixed form of payment varied from the traditional one-sixth royalty to larger and smaller royalties, sliding scale royalties, or net profit-shares, the cash bonus was always retained as the bid variable. The U.S. Supreme Court ruled in December 1981 that the Interior Department was not in violation of the 1978 amendments.
30. 43 U.S.C.A. 1344(a).

OCS "in a manner which considers economic, social, and environmental values of the renewable and non-renewable resources contained therein."[31] An ambitious five-year leasing plan was prepared by former Interior Secretary James Watt. This plan was substantially amended by his successor, William Clark.

Lessees are required to prepare and submit exploration plans to the Secretary for approval.[32] The Secretary is empowered to require modifications of these plans, as deemed necessary, to achieve consistency with the provisions of the act and any regulations subsequently issued under the act.[33] These modifications are to be exercised after bidding has been completed and leases have been issued. After exploration begins, the Secretary is empowered to order a suspension or temporary prohibition of any exploration activities and to require preparation of a revised exploration plan.[34] He may also require any lessee operating under an approved exploration plan to obtain a permit prior to drilling.[35]

As an additional planning step, the legislation requires that each lessee submit a development and production plan to the Interior Secretary for approval.[36] This plan must describe all facilities and operations that will be utilized in development and production of oil and gas from the lease area.[37] The description must include the location and size of such facilities as well as the land, labor, materials, and energy requirements associated with such facilities, and all environmental and safety measures to be implemented.[38]

3. Responding to demands from coastal states, the role of state and local government officials in planning for lease sales, exploration, and development has been considerably expanded. The five-year leasing plan must be submitted to the governor of each affected state for review and comment.[39] Any comments that request a modification require a written reply by the Interior Secretary.[40] All such correspondence must then be submitted to Congress with the proposed

---

31. Id. 1344(a)(1).
32. Id. 1340(c)(1).
33. Id.
34. 43 U.S.C.A. 1340(f)(1).
35. Id. 1340(f).
36. Id. 1351(a)(1).
37. Id. 1351(a)(2).
38. Id.
39. 43 U.S.C.A. 1344(c)(2).
40. Id.

plan.[41] The legislation further mandates that "the Secretary shall accept recommendations of the governor" if the Secretary determines that they provide a reasonable balance between the national interest and the well-being of the citizens of the affected state.[42] Consultation with and recommendations from officials of local government jurisdictions are also encouraged and solicited, but the Secretary is not constrained to accept these recommendations, as is the case with recommendations by governors.[43] For the newly required exploration and production plans, the legislation specifies that the Secretary shall not grant a license or a permit for any activity affecting land use or water use in the coastal zone of a state unless the state agrees that the activity does not conflict with any approved coastal zone management plan.[44]

4. Following a precedent established in administration of the oil import quota system, the federal government has increasingly used its power to favor small as opposed to large refiners. The 1978 legislation expands this "small refiner bias" by mandating that every oil or gas lease require the lessee to offer to sell 20 percent of his oil and gas production to small or independent refiners at market value.[45] While other legislation defines the small or independent refiner, the difficulty of determining market value in specific cases is acknowledged in the legislation.[46] When arm's-length market value evidence is not available, the Interior Secretary is authorized to determine an appropriate price.[47]

5. The 1978 legislation also provides funds to compensate injured economic interests for damages arising out of oil spills or other activities related to oil and gas production from the OCS. The act creates an Offshore Oil Pollution Compensation Fund in an amount not to exceed $200 million.[48] This fund is to be financed by a fee of not more than 3 cents per barrel of oil produced from the OCS, and is imposed on the lessee at the point of production.[49] The fund is to become immediately available to compensate for oil spill removal

41. Id.
42. 43 U.S.C.A. 1345(c).
43. Id.
44. 16 U.S.C.A. 1456(3)(Supp. 1979); 43 U.S.C.A. 1351(d)(Supp. 1979).
45. 43 U.S.C.A. 1337(b)(7)(Supp. 1979).
46. Id. 1331(o).
47. Id.
48. 43 U.S.C.A. 1812(a).
49. Id. 1812(d)(1).

costs, the processing and settlement of claims, and all administrative and personnel costs borne by the federal government arising out of oil spills.[50]

In addition, a Fisherman's Contingency Fund in an amount not to exceed $1 million is created.[51] Again the fund is to be financed by a levy on lessees in an amount to be specified by the Secretary of the Interior.[52] The purpose of the fund is to provide compensation for damages to fishing gear and for any economic loss to commercial fishermen due to activities related to oil and gas exploration or production.

Creation of these funds increases the probability that damaged parties will be compensated without resorting to litigation. The fees will tend to internalize the external costs of oil spills and other damages associated with OCS oil production.

6. Critics of the 1953 OCS Lands Act have made the argument that since the federal government has no exploration and drilling program of its own, it is placed in a position of not knowing the value of the oil and gas leases that it is required to sell. Proposals for a mandatory government exploration program were not included in the amended act, but a new section was inserted requiring that lessees shall provide the Interior Secretary access to all data and information (including processed, analyzed, and interpreted information) obtained from any exploration, development, or production activity on federal leases.[54] State governments have access to this information when it is relevant to their state. No private parties, except those who have carried the costs of producing the data, have access to the information. The Secretary is required to make such information available to the affected states.[55] The Secretary is also required to prescribe regulations designed to maintain confidentiality of privileged or proprietary information from lessees.[56] Civil action for damages may be instituted against any federal or state government employee who supplies confidential information to an unauthorized person.[57]

50. Id. 1812(c).
51. Id. 1812(c).
52. Id. 1842(a).
53. Id. 1843(c)(1).
54. Id. 1352(a)(1)(A).
55. Id. 1352(b)(2).
56. Id. 1352(c).
57. Id. 1352(f)(1).

Oil companies vigorously resisted this part of the legislation on the grounds that such proprietary information is paid for by lessees and is a valuable asset.[58] The legislation created a serious risk of loss of valuable assets without hope of compensation, implying a disincentive for certain types of expensive drilling programs.

RECENT DEVELOPMENTS

As noted above, in the 1978 amendments Congress mandated that alternative, nontraditional bidding systems be used for between 20 and 60 percent of the offshore acreage leased over a five-year trial period. The trial period ended in September 1983, and the legislation guiding offshore leasing bidding systems has reverted to the 1953 act. In a report to Congress, the U.S. General Accounting Office makes the following recommendation:

> Because of the long lead-time between the award of a lease and exploration, and the uncertainties associated with actually finding oil and gas, [GAO] recommends that the Congress amend the OCS Lands Act to require continued use of alternatives to the cash bonus, fixed royalty bidding system in leasing offshore lands for another 5-year period.[59]

As of July 1984, their recommendation has not been acted upon.

Another recent development has been the move by the Reagan administration toward giving coastal states a larger portion of the revenue from OCS leasing. At present, coastal states receive only a small share of lease revenues. States are also entitled to a portion of the revenues from federal leases that are located near state waters; however, these funds are tied up in litigation. It is the apparent hope of the administration that sharing the revenues of offshore oil and gas development will reduce opposition to federal offshore leasing plans.[60]

58. See statements by oil company executives in *Hearings Before the Ad Hoc Select Committee on Outer Continental Shelf on H.R. 1614,* 95th Congress, 1st Session 1444 (1977).

59. U.S. General Accounting Office, Comptroller General's Report to Congress, *Congress Should Extend Mandate to Experiment with Alternative Bidding Systems in Leasing Offshore Lands,* GAO/RCED-83-139, 27 May 1983, p. vi.

60. See Andy Pasztor, "Reagan Moving Toward Giving States Larger Share of Offshore Leasing Money," *Wall Street Journal,* 13 June 1984, p. 15.

2

THE ECONOMIC MEANING OF CONSERVATION

In this chapter we establish the theoretical framework for studying the effectiveness of government policies in managing the Outer Continental Shelf. The discussion begins with an analysis of widely accepted interpretations of the meaning of the term *conservation* and identifies several shortcomings in these conceptions. We then offer an alternative economic definition of conservation and discuss the implications of this definition for natural resource production and consumption. Next, we describe the circumstances under which a market-oriented economy will or will not naturally conserve resources, and we discuss what economic policies (if any) may be adopted to enhance resource conservation. Finally, we discuss the implications of the economic definition of conservation for the distribution of income in society.

ECONOMICS AND RESOURCE CONSERVATION

Economics is the social science that deals with the allocation and distribution of scarce resources. A resource is scarce if the amount that is freely available is less than that which is desired or demanded by society at a zero price. The existence of scarcity requires that difficult choices must be made among competing alternative uses, and this raises some fundamental questions: What criteria should apply in deciding the use of a nation's natural resources? When are they to be used? Who will enjoy their benefits? Economists sum up the answer to these questions as follows: We should conserve our natural resources.

There is nearly unanimous agreement on the wisdom of this statement, but there is widespread disagreement on what actually constitutes conservation. Conservation is derived from the latin word *conservare,* which means to keep or to preserve. In its modern meaning, conservation is synonymous with safeguarding resources, keeping them from being damaged or wasted, and preserving or saving them for the future. These definitions seem to imply that resources are conserved if we reduce current consumption. For example, forests are conserved by recycling paper (although resources expended in the recycling process are not). Petroleum is conserved by obeying the 55-mile-per-hour speed limit (but human resources expended in increased driving time are not). The "using less" definition of conservation is logically flawed. Carried to the extreme, it implies that perfect conservation is achieved when no natural resources are used and all resources are hoarded. Furthermore, using less of one resource may require increased use of other resources—an eventuality that may not be desirable. If our natural resources are to provide value to society, they must ultimately be utilized and enjoyed. We therefore need a definition of conservation that acknowledges the trade-offs between current and future consumption and considers impacts on other affected resources.

The alternative definition of conservation put forth by economists recognizes these trade-offs. It requires that resources be used in such a way that their value to both current and future generations is maximized. Resource value is computed by taking into account (1) society's willingness to pay for the resource (reflected in its market price), (2) the social costs of producing the resource, and (3) society's evaluation of future versus current consumption. At times, the economic definition of conservation is consistent with the "using less" definition discussed above. However, in some instances this alternative definition may imply exactly the opposite—more resources should be used today and less tomorrow.

In its economic conception, conservation has both intra- and intertemporal aspects. The intratemporal aspect focuses on resource management within a specific time period, or minimizing the current period costs of a certain level of economic activity, while the intertemporal aspect is concerned with finding the optimal time pattern of economic activity. In the case of oil and gas deposits, decisions regarding the proper level of current production have direct implications for future production. For example, if the rate of extraction from an offshore oil lease is increased today, this necessarily reduces the amount of future production. Although intra- and intertemporal decisions are closely intertwined, the two are discussed separately below for expositional ease.

INTRATEMPORAL CONSERVATION—RESOURCE MANAGEMENT WHEN TIME DOES NOT MATTER

Within any given time period, resource conservation requires that we maximize the economic rent that can be derived from a resource. The concept of economic rent was first set forth by David Ricardo in his studies of the role of agricultural land in a nation's growth. Today, economic rent is defined as the payment to a resource in excess of that necessary to keep it in its current use. This is expressed as follows:

$$Rent = Revenue - Cost$$

Revenue is defined as the price of the resource as determined in a competitive market, P, multiplied by the quantity of the resource that is produced, Q. The total social cost of production, often called the opportunity cost, is the sum of the values of the resources used in the production of output in their best alternative use. In the case of exhaustible resources, the opportunity cost of production includes the value of the lost opportunity to produce the same output units in the future. This latter cost represents a portion of the connection between intra- and intertemporal conservation. The observation that opportunity costs are never zero is the source of the well-known saying, "There is no such thing as a free lunch."

The source of economic rent stems from control over some input factor with superior productivity. Ricardo's analysis was concerned with rent earned on land parcels of differing quality. He showed that as production increases and existing labor and capital are used more intensively, additional increments to output become more and more expensive. This is a consequence of the famous "law of diminishing returns." But the same reasoning can be applied to inputs in general and mineral deposits in particular. For example, production costs for oil in the Middle East may be as low as 50 cents per barrel, whereas the world market price is currently about $30 per barrel. The difference between the two is accounted for by economic rent.

The typical revenue and cost relationships are illustrated in Figure 2–1.

The revenue curve, R, is assumed to be linear, reflecting the fact that output prices are fixed to an individual producer. The S-shaped cost curve, C, reflects the increasing costs of production described above. It

Figure 2-1. Typical Revenue and Cost Curves.

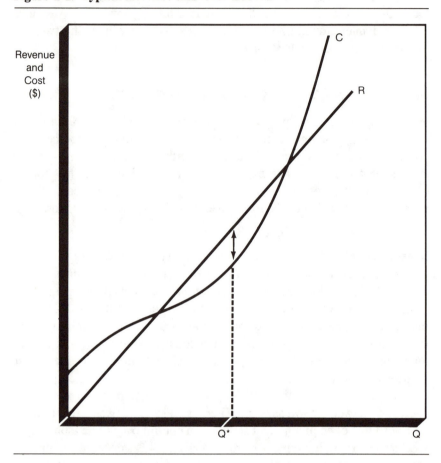

is implicit in the cost curve that production proceeds at the minimum possible cost for any given level of output. Economic rent maximization requires the selection of a level of output such that the vertical distance between these two curves is the greatest. This occurs in Figure 2-1 at output level Q^*.

Output level Q^* can be found in two ways. First, it can be found by inspecting the revenue and cost curves and calculating the economic rent for every conceivable level of output. Although this method will ultimately result in the proper level of output, it is slow and tedious. Alternatively, Q^* can be found by using an incremental or marginalist approach. Starting with a small level of output, one would ask whether the social benefits of another unit of production exceed the social costs. The value that society places on one more unit of output is summarized by the price that individuals are willing to pay for that output. The social opportunity cost incurred in producing an additional unit of output is given by its marginal cost, *MC*. Conservation of resources is attained when the value society places on the last unit of output, its price, is equated to the marginal social opportunity cost of the productive inputs. If price exceeds marginal cost, conservation is served by expanding the production of that good. Alternatively, if the marginal cost of a resource exceeds its price, society is best served by reducing the production of that resource. These incremental benefits and costs are illustrated in Figure 2–2.[1]

Figure 2–2. Incremental Benefits and Costs, and Rent Maximization.

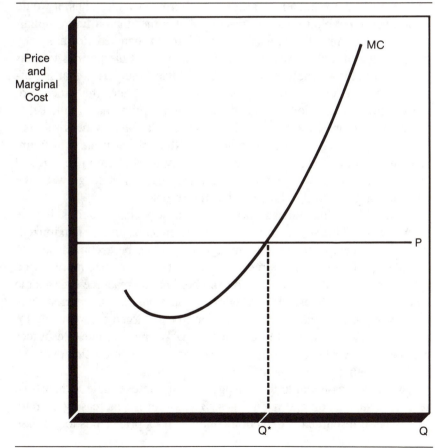

1. The analysis above is based on the assumption that private benefits (revenues) and private costs are identical to social benefits and costs. A discussion of whether a market economy will lead to such results is undertaken in a later section of this chapter.

In summary, economic rent is maximized, and conservation is served, by equating the price of a competitively produced product, *P,* to its social marginal cost, *MC,* which is shown at output level Q^*.

INTERTEMPORAL CONSERVATION—RESOURCE MANAGEMENT WHEN TIME MATTERS

Socially, we are not only faced with the decision of how much to produce, but also with the decision of when to produce. In order to time resource development optimally, the net benefits of current production must be compared to those of future production. However, intertemporal dollar values cannot be compared directly because a dollar received today can be invested at current interest rates and will grow in value. Thus, it would always be preferable to have a present dollar rather than a future dollar.

This intertemporal comparison problem is handled formally by transforming all dollar values received in different time periods to their equivalent value in one time period. The single time period that is nor- mally selected for the comparison is the present, and the process of transforming future dollars into their present equivalent is called dis- counting. The present time period equivalent of a future sum is referred to as its present value. The computation of the present value of a future sum amounts to asking what amount of money would have to be invested today, at current market interest rates, in order for it to grow to the specified future sum by the specified future date.[2]

Economic rent maximization (resource conservation) requires that the present value of the stream of net revenues from a resource be maximized. As with intratemporal rent maximization, this can be accomplished in- crementally. Production of a resource should be delayed one more period if the rate of growth of net revenue from holding the resource exceeds the market rate of interest. By delaying production for one period, one forgoes the interest income that could have been earned by producing to- day and investing the net revenue at the market interest rate. Resources are conserved when no possible rearrangement of the production path will lead to a higher present value.

This idea is essential to the management of nonrenewable, exhaustible resources such as oil and natural gas. Because of the increasing scarcity of a mineral resource (as depletion continues), its price tends to increase

---

2. For a more detailed discussion of discounting, see J. Fred Weston and Eugene F. Brigham, *Managerial Finance,* 6th ed. (Hinsdale, Ill.: Dryden Press, 1978), pp. 249–82.

over time at a faster rate than do production costs.[3] Thus the value of an oil and gas resource *in situ* (in the ground) will tend to rise over time. One portion of the opportunity cost of producing oil and natural gas today is the expected appreciation of the resource if it is left in the ground for one more time period. In the final evaluation, resources are conserved when the rate of growth of net revenue (or alternatively, the rate of growth of the *in situ* value of the resource) is equal to the interest rate.

INTRA– AND INTERTEMPORAL CONSERVATION SUMMARIZED

It is not strictly correct to isolate the intratemporal from the intertemporal aspect of conservation. The relationship between inter- and intratemporal conservation is summarized in Figure 2–3.

Because the amount of revenue (and cost) derived from the resource will vary depending on when the resource is produced, all values illustrated in the diagram are expressed in present values. The total area shown in Figure 2–3 represents the present value of gross revenue from a resource. The shaded area represents the present value of the total necessary costs of bringing the resource to market. This includes a normal rate of return on invested capital for the developer, which is properly considered to be an opportunity cost of production. The remaining unshaded area in Figure 2–3 is the economic rent.

Resource conservation is equivalent to maximizing the present value of economic rent. If for any reason natural resources are developed too quickly (or too slowly), the resource is not conserved. Referring to Figure 2–3, suboptimal timing of resource development and production reduces the size of the rectangle representing total gross revenue and therefore the rectangle representing economic rent.[4] Similarly, if production costs are not minimized relative to the revenue flow, the size of the rectangle representing necessary cost grows without a commensurate growth in total gross revenue. The net result is a reduction in economic rent.

There are other ways in which resources may be wasted. For example, if a resource is not allocated to its highest and best use, or if government regulations impose unnecessarily high administrative and/or compliance costs on the producer, conservation is not attained. These kinds of

---

3. See Harold Hotelling, "The Economics of Exhaustible Resources," *Journal of Political Economy* 39 (no. 2, April 1931): 137–75.

4. The suboptimal timing of production can alternatively be thought of as reducing the net present value of a resource *in situ*.

Figure 2–3. An Illustration of Economic Rent.

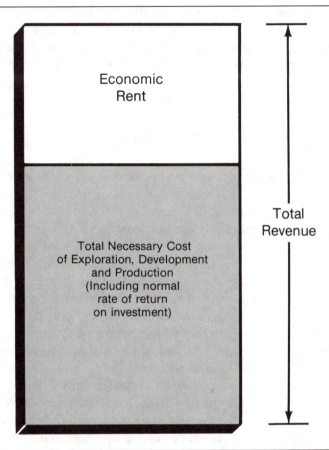

Source: Derived from R. O. Jones, Walter J. Mead, and Philip E. Sorensen, "The Outer Continental Shelf Lands Act Amendments of 1978," *Natural Resources Journal* 19 (Oct. 1979).

Note: All flows are net present values.

resource waste are seldom acknowledged in the writings of those espousing the noneconomic view of conservation.

THE PRIVATE MARKET AND RESOURCE CONSERVATION

One of the fundamental propositions in economics is that private market resource allocation, under appropriate conditions, will coincide with resource conservation. This idea was first put forth in 1776 by Adam Smith in his classic treatise, *The Wealth of Nations.* Smith argued that in a market economy, individual decision-makers are guided as if by an "invisible hand" to promote resource conservation. In his own words:

> As every individual, therefore, endeavors as much as he can to employ his capital in support of domestic industry that its produce may be of the greatest value; every individual necessarily labors to render the annual revenue of the society as great as he can. He generally, indeed, neither intends to promote the public interest, nor knows how much he is promoting it. . . . He intends only his own security; and by directing that industry in such a manner as its produce may be of the greatest value, he intends only his own gain, and he is in this, as in other cases, led by an invisible hand to promote an end which was no part of his intention. . . . By pursuing his own interest he frequently promotes that of society more effectively than when he really intends to promote it.[5]

Economists have constructed elaborate theoretical models based on the insights presented by Adam Smith to determine the set of conditions under which a market allocation of resources will be consistent with resource conservation. A market that meets these conditions is referred to as perfectly competitive. In theory, a perfectly competitive market is characterized by a large number of buyers and sellers trading a homogeneous product. All market participants have access to perfect information about all relevant trading opportunities and can move freely in and out of the industry. Under these conditions, the market price established by the interaction of profit-maximizing sellers and utility-maximizing buyers will necessarily equal marginal costs. In other words, a perfectly competitive market conserves resources and promotes the common good.

Of course, no industry in the real world satisfies the theoretical conditions for perfect competition. As far as a particular industry is concerned, the relevant empirical question is whether there are circumstances present that will cause the market allocation of resources to systematically deviate from the perfectly competitive (resource conserving) solution over a relatively long period of time. This is one of the questions that will be addressed in subsequent chapters.

THE NATURE OF MARKET FAILURES

The discussion in the previous section makes it clear that a freely adjusting market price is a valuable tool for conserving resources. The

5. Adam Smith, *An Inquiry into the Nature and Causes of the Wealth of Nations,* 1776 (New York: Random House, Modern Library, 1937), p. 423.

market price of a resource summarizes substantial quantities of information about the commodity. Under competitive conditions, it simultaneously reveals both the nature of consumer preferences and the cost conditions of the sellers. However, when market prices do not reveal this information, markets cannot be relied upon to conserve resources. Unfortunately, this can occur under a number of different circumstances.

Lack of Competition

If an individual or coalition of individuals of either buyers or sellers comprise a large enough portion of a market to manipulate the market price, and if these individuals choose to exercise this power, the market allocation of resources will not be consistent with conservation. A market structure that allows a single seller to manipulate market prices is called a *monopoly* (or in the case of a coalition of a few sellers, *oligopoly)*. Its counterpart, with market power concentrated on the buyer's side, is called *monopsony* (or in the case of a coalition of a few buyers, *oligopsony)*. Monopolies exploit buyers by charging a price for their product in excess of its marginal cost. This results in a level of production that is less than the socially desirable level. Similarly, monopsonies exploit sellers by paying a price that is less than the competitive price and buying less than is socially desirable. Monopolies and monopsonies can only exist in the long run when there are barriers to entry into the industry that restrict resource mobility or when government interferes with the price setting mechanism.

If a seller sets prices that are above the competitive level and that yield profits beyond the normal rate of return, other firms will soon enter the industry, when possible. The new entrants will drive down the price of the product, returning the rate of return to the competitive level. Similarly, if a buyer sets prices below the competitive level and there are no barriers restricting entry, other buyers will move into the market, bidding up the price of the good to the competitive level.

Superficially, the OCS lease market appears to have elements of both monopoly and oligopsony. The government is the sole supplier of OCS leases in the United States and can raise prices by deliberately slowing down the rate at which new leases are offered for development. However, this strategy could succeed only if U.S. petroleum prices increased in response to lower offshore production. The higher petroleum prices would lead participants in OCS auctions to raise their bids. The net effect would be a transfer of income from petroleum consumers to the beneficiaries of increased government income, with OCS bidders acting as income transfer agents. The idea that the government should attempt to exercise a monopoly strategy has never been seriously suggested because it does not make sense economically or politically. While the offshore area provides a significant portion of total U.S. production, the effect that such a government strategy would have on worldwide crude oil prices is not large enough to warrant such a strategy. Most recently, the federal government has been criticized for offering leases too rapidly. But the argument of the critics has not been that the government should slow leasing to realize monopoly profits. Rather, the criticism comes from concern about the environmental effects of offshore production and doubts that the OCS industry has the capacity effectively to explore as much acreage as is being offered, given the five-year primary lease term.

The buyer's side of the OCS market has been described by some as oligopsonistic because relatively few firms participate in offshore lease auctions. It is sometimes further argued that the large capital outlays necessary to participate in this market are an effective barrier to entry for small firms. If true, actual participants in OCS auctions could profit at the expense of the public by paying prices that are too low for the leases they acquire. Others have argued that even with the participation of relatively few firms, OCS lease auctions are still effectively competitive. These conflicting hypotheses are tested in Chapter 3.

The most effective (and possibly the only effective) monopoly power observed in the U.S. oil market since the dissolution of the Rockefeller Standard Oil Company in 1911 has been through government intervention. The system of market demand prorationing introduced in the mid-1930s and effectively abandoned in 1972 used the power of government to force producers to reduce output, thereby causing crude oil prices to be higher than competitive behavior would permit. Another illustration is provided by the mandatory oil import quota system introduced by the federal government in 1959 and abandoned in 1972. This system restricted competing oil supplies from imports and again caused crude oil and petroleum product prices in the United States to rise above competitive levels.

Externalities

If market prices do not reflect the full social costs or benefits of a commodity, an externality or spillover is present. Under these circumstances, markets will fail to conserve resources. Externalities can be either positive or negative. A positive externality exists when the social benefits of an activity exceed the private benefits. In the presence of positive spillovers, the private market will tend to produce too little of a product.

The reason for this market failure is that individual decision-makers consider private rather than social benefits and costs when deciding how much of an activity to undertake. This decision can be cast in the marginalist framework. An activity is expanded as long as *private* marginal benefits exceed *private* marginal costs. However, in the case of a positive externality, because social benefits exceed the private benefits, an individual acting in his own interest cannot take advantage of all opportunities that are in the interest of society.[6]

As an example of a positive externality from OCS leasing, consider the information derived from exploring a lease tract. This information not only provides a benefit to the firm that undertakes the exploration; it also conveys benefits to the owners of neighboring tracts. If oil is found, the likelihood that oil is present on an adjacent tract increases, and the value of that tract is raised. Even if the exploratory well is not successful, benefits will be conferred on the neighboring operators who may be able to save costly exploration efforts. This issue has been the source of legal contention.

Negative externalities are said to exist when the private costs of production understate the social costs of production. Under these circumstances, the market will tend to produce too much of a product. This will occur because individuals consider *private* rather than social costs in making private decisions. They do not consider that their actions may have costs that are borne by others. As a consequence, economic activity is carried beyond the point of resource conservation, that is, beyond the point where social marginal benefits and costs are equated.[7]

The obvious example of a negative externality relating to OCS development is oil spills, as exemplified by the Santa Barbara experience referred to in Chapter 1. This spill prompted the Department of the Interior to review the ecological impact on the marine environment from continued OCS oil and gas operations. One outcome of this review has been a costly regulatory burden on the industry. However, since 1969 no major oil spill has occurred in the United States as a result of offshore oil development.[8]

---

6. For a more detailed explanation of market failures due to externalities, see James Gwartney and Richard Stroup, *Economics: Private and Public Choice* (Orlando, Fla.: Academic Press, 1983).

7. Ibid.

8. For an analysis of the Santa Barbara experience, see Walter J. Mead and Philip E. Sorensen, "The Economic Cost of the Santa Barbara Oil Spill," in *Santa Barbara Oil Spill: An Environmental Inquiry*, University of California at Santa Barbara, California Marine Science Institute, Santa Barbara, 1972. Most oil spills are not related to offshore drilling but, rather, to transportation of oil by tanker. See, for example, U.S. Department of Commerce and National Oceanic and Atmospheric Administration, *Assessing the Social Costs of Oil Spills: The AMOCO-CADIZ Case Study*, July 1983.

Another negative externality sometimes present in offshore activities results from the physical and legal attributes of oil and gas ownership. Oil and gas are migratory resources that are subject to the "rule of capture." This means that oil and natural gas belong to the individual who extracts the resource from the ground. This is true even if the oil that is extracted from a particular onshore tract has in fact been drained from a neighboring tract. Under present laws, the party at loss is not entitled to compensation.

If a reservoir is subject to drainage from several independent operators, each operator has an incentive to produce as much as possible, as quickly as possible. The consequence is a rapid reduction in the natural geological pressures that drive the oil and gas to the surface. This ultimately reduces the total recovery from the reservoir. In this way the activities of one operator impose external costs on the other operators who have an economic interest in the reservoir.

In the case of offshore OCS oil and gas, the rule of capture has been modified by recent legislation and federal court litigation. The Outer Continental Shelf Lands Act Amendments of 1978, Section 8(f), required the federal government as the lessor to pay some of its bonus, royalty, and other lease revenues into a fund subject to a "fair and equitable" distribution between the federal and adjacent state governments. The lands subject to payments into the funds were identified as those lying within three miles of the seaward boundaries of the adjacent coastal states. The critical paragraph of the statute is as follows:

> The Secretary shall deposit in a separate account in the Treasury of the United States all bonus, royalties, and other revenues attributable to oil and gas pools underlying both the outer Continental Shelf and Submerged lands subject to the jurisdiction of any coastal state until such time as the Secretary and the Governor of such coastal State agree on, or . . . a district court of the United States determines, the fair and equitable disposition of such revenues and any interest which has accrued . . . .

Thus, any drainage from adjacent state lands would require compensation from the federal government. No state has passed similar legislation requiring that it pay the federal government in the event that drainage adversely affects the value of federal leases.

A federal judge in Texas recently decided that "disposition of federal lease revenue, pursuant to Section 8 (g) (4), is not limited to compensation for drainage."[9] The court decided that the federal government must

---

9. Civil Action No. B-79-476-CA, *State of Texas v. Secretary of the Interior, et al.*, p. 5.

also share with the state bonus payments that were "enhanced" by virtue of oil discoveries on prior and adjacent state tracts. The court was silent on the more common possibility—that dry holes on adjacent state tracts might lead to lower bonus payments on adjacent and subsequently leased federal lands, or to no bonus payments at all. In any event, the rule of capture has now been modified in the case of federal OCS leases sharing the same reservoir with adjacent states.

In the final analysis, the problem of externalities is a problem of undefined or unenforceable property rights. When the air or water is polluted, it is because no one owns these resources. Problems with spillover benefits occur because the producer of these benefits is unable to appropriate the value generated for others. One way to internalize externalities is to define property rights in such a way that they are enforceable at a relatively low cost. If, in addition, transaction costs are low, markets can still be effective in allocating resources.[10]

Asymmetrical Distribution of Information

One assumption of perfect competition is that participants are equally well informed. The market may fail to yield competitive results if this assumption is not met.

It has long been recognized in the literature that the OCS lease market may fail to yield competitive outcomes because of certain peculiarities present at the exploration stage. Prior to a sale, potential bidders engage in extensive exploration activities to determine which tracts are of interest and to develop a bidding strategy. Kash et al. have made a distinction between three major phases in exploration and have given a description of the activities in each phase.

In phase one, regional surveys are conducted to identify promising geological formations, mostly by gravitational and magnetic measurements. Phase two consists of detailed surveys of specific tracts, including seismic surveys and sampling of materials from the seabed (bottom sampling) and from below the seabed (coring). Phase three is the culmination of exploration efforts: A well is drilled to determine whether oil and gas are present.[11]

10. This idea was first discussed by Ronald Coase in his classic article, "The Problem of Social Cost," *Journal of Law and Economics* 3 (Oct. 1960): 1–44.

11. D. E. Kash, et al., *Energy Under the Oceans* (Norman: University of Oklahoma Press, 1973), pp. 26–47.

The data collected in each phase are considered proprietary by the industry. The industry's philosophy is succinctly stated in the following quotation from an *Oil and Gas Journal* editorial:

> The geological and geophysical data plus the company's own structural interpretations based on this data are amassed at heavy cost. They are closely guarded, and disclosure would hurt a company's competitive position.[12]

When areas where drilling experience is lacking (i.e., wildcat acreage) are offered for lease, potential bidders are limited to the phase-two type of exploration. No on-structure well drilling is allowed on tracts offered for sale. Companies often form coalitions to collect geophysical data on wildcat leases. Seismic data may be obtained through a "group shoot" (a contract between several companies and a single geophysical contracting firm). The companies share the cost of the survey and the survey data. Gaskins and Teisberg note that "the value of basic geophysical data by itself is apparently quite small. It is the interpretation of the data that produces useful information about the lease values."[13] The strategic value of information gained from geophysical data interpretation is shown in the fact that such information "is invariably a closely guarded secret for each prospective bidder."[14]

The situation is quite different when tracts are offered for sale in areas where nearby leases have already been substantially explored through well drilling. Companies operating nearby leases have the advantage of being able to complement geophysical information with well-drilling and production data from nearby tracts when estimating the value of the tracts offered for sale.[15] In this case, information will be asymmetrically distributed between potential bidders because of differing opportunities for collecting data.

The most extreme case of information advantage occurs when a bidder ("the neighbor") has access to data from wells drilled on an adjacent tract locating a reservoir that (on the basis of geophysical information) is believed to extend into the tract offered for sale. Even though non-

12. "Industry's Only Course: Fight the New Offshore Rules," editorial in *The Oil and Gas Journal,* 4 Aug. 1969, p. 75.

13. D. W. Gaskins, Jr. and T. Teisberg, "An Economic Analysis of Pre-Sale Exploration in Oil and Gas Lease Sales," in R. T. Masson and P. D. Qualls, eds., *Essays in Industrial Organization in Honor of Joe S. Bain* (Cambridge, Mass.: Ballinger Publishing Company, 1976), p. 243.

14. Ibid., p. 244.

15. D. S. Holland, "The Energy Search—Gulf of Mexico," *Exploration and Economics of the Petroleum Industry,* vol. 14 (Los Angeles: Matthew Bender & Co., 1976), pp. 51–61.

neighbors generally know whether a well has been successful or not in locating a reservoir on the neighboring tract, the neighbor retains his advantage through exclusive knowledge of important reservoir parameters. These include data on the gas-oil ratio, reservoir pressure, the thickness of the reservoir, and the quality of the oil. This knowledge enables the neighbor to evaluate more accurately than any non-neighbor the value of reserves under the adjacent tract.

Even though the Department of the Interior recognizes the advantages of adjacent lessees in bidding for leases, the disclosure rules for exploratory data received from lessees have not been used to eliminate these advantages.[16] Historically, the DOI has accepted the argument that exploring firms have a property right to the information they acquire, and thus the bidding advantages. But the length of time for which this right is in effect has been reduced. Before 1976, exploratory information received from OCS lessees was not made available for public inspection without the consent of the lessee unless the lease was relinquished or it was determined to be necessary for the proper development of a nearby field.

In June of 1976, a rule was introduced that provided for disclosure of geological data of analyzed (but not interpreted) geological information two years after they have been received by the USGS or on relinquishment of the lease, whichever comes first. It is not likely that this provision will affect bidding behavior for drainage tracts because of the policy of leasing such tracts rapidly in order to prevent drainage of unleased lands.

The strategic importance of superior information is evident in the following observations reported in the *Oil and Gas Journal:*

> Some of the companies bidding have leases with producing wells offsetting the tracts up for sale. These companies have been extremely careful not to let any information leak out about the offset wells. Competing companies have only the well locations and the seismograph pictures to guide them. Thus the companies with offsetting production are in the best position to judge the value of the lease.[17]

Whether or not superior information actually allows the neighbor to profit by buying leases from the federal government at less than a competitive price is an empirical question addressed in Chapter 3.

---

16. Disclosure rules for data received from OCS lessees are contained in 30 C.F.R., 250.9.

17. "Offshore Sale Again Breaks Records," *The Oil and Gas Journal,* 17 Aug. 1959, p. 91.

CORRECTING MARKET FAILURES

The correction of market failures resulting from inadequate competition, externalities, or asymmetrical information is one of the major economic justifications and functions of government. The actual means of correction used by government vary, depending upon the type of market failure encountered. No general agreement exists among economists, politicians, or administrators about the efficacy of government activity in this area.

For example, the market failures associated with insufficient competition have been the subject of considerable controversy. As a result of the belief by some that competition for offshore leases is inadequate, steps have been taken to improve the competitive position of smaller firms. One step in this direction is the ban on joint bids submitted by a coalition including more than one of the nine firms producing more than 1.6 million barrels of oil per day worldwide. The effects of these policies are discussed in Chapter 3.

Another attempt to improve competition has been the movement away from the bonus bid as the bid variable at OCS auctions. The large size of the bonus bid, which averaged $2.2 million for the 1,223 Gulf of Mexico leases issued from 1954 through 1969, may act as a barrier to entry to smaller firms. It is often argued that bidding systems in which payments to the government are contingent on commercial resource findings (e.g., royalty and profit share bidding systems) are superior to bonus bidding in this respect. These alternative bid variables require little if any "up front" money and may enhance competition. They are analyzed in Chapter 4.

Market failures that occur as a result of externalities are generally treated by government action that requires the firm to internalize the spillovers. This can be accomplished in a number of ways. For example, consider the "common property" problem (discussed earlier), which occurs when there are multiple owners of an oil field. This problem can be solved through a practice known as *unitization*. When a field is unitized, the owners select an operator to manage the field. The unit operator maximizes the profit from the field and shares the proceeds with the other owners on a predetermined basis. If the unitization is structured properly, the combined profits of the parties to the agreement will be maximized and the resource conserved. Another method for dealing with externalities is through a system of standards and fines. Ideally, the government agency in charge of this activity would estimate the marginal social benefits and costs of the spillover activity and would formulate a legal standard. If the standard is violated, a fine is imposed on the offending party. Setting and enforcing this standard can attain resource conservation. An example of this method is the air pollution standards imposed on offshore producers.

The primary method chosen by the federal government to correct for the common property characteristics of oil is to determine a level of output for each nonexempt well and to require a producer to limit his production to the prescribed allowable rate. This system aims at a "maximum efficient rate" of production (MER). However, the use of rules of thumb (rather than an appropriate economic rationale) plus a host of politically expedient exemptions have caused the system to deviate widely from the standard of resource conservation.[18]

There are many ways of dealing with market failure. In general, economists advocate methods designed to give private decision-makers an incentive to act in the public interest. But the government often opts for methods that rely upon extensive government policing of the private sector, forcing society to bear unnecessary, high costs. For example, in the standards and fines approach to correcting externalities, the costs of monitoring an activity may be higher than the benefits yielded to society by the monitoring.

Another problem of government intervention stems from the nature of the political process. It is to be expected that once the government has established a set of regulations governing a particular activity, individuals will act in a fashion to minimize the negative effects and maximize the positive effects of these rules. In fact, it is to be expected that individuals will utilize the political arena to further their own well-being, sometimes at the expense of society in general.

Regardless of the approach that is decided on to solve a market failure, the resulting policy should be submitted to the rigors of benefit-cost analysis, and only policies that render a net social benefit should be implemented. This is seldom done. Although market failures may lead to a waste of resources, the costs of government policies in this area are sometimes higher than the social costs of the market failure.

THE PROBLEM OF INCOME DISTRIBUTION

Conservation, as defined by economists, does not address the problem of income distribution. The definition is based on the idea that the present

18. For a thorough review of the present conservation regulations system and a criticism from an economic perspective, see Stephen L. McDonald, *Petroleum Conservation in the United States: An Economic Analysis* (Baltimore: Johns Hopkins University Press, 1971), especially part 3.

value of total social wealth should be maximized. It has little to say about how wealth should be distributed among the members of society. Nevertheless, much of the controversy regarding offshore policy centers on this issue. One of the reasons that coastal states like California have recently opposed federal offshore leasing adjacent to their shores is that such jurisdictions receive few benefits from these activities and yet must bear a disproportionate percentage of their costs. In the case of federal offshore leases, the revenue derived at the auctions—and all subsequent revenue collected in the form of rental and royalty payments—accrues principally to the federal government. However, the costs associated with an increased probability of an oil spill or additional air pollution are mostly borne by the coastal residents.[19] Although it may be obvious that offshore oil and gas development is beneficial from a social viewpoint, this mismatching of benefits and costs (an income distribution issue) may keep offshore leasing from proceeding at the socially optimal rate.

19. The Offshore Oil Pollution Compensation Fund created by the OCS Lands Act Amendments of 1978 helps to offset the costs of oil spills.

3

AN ANALYSIS OF THE EFFECTIVENESS OF BONUS BIDDING FOR ISSUING OCS OIL AND GAS LEASES

The dominant system for leasing Outer Continental Shelf lands for oil and gas development has been cash bonus bidding with a fixed royalty rate of 16⅔ percent of production value (or quantity). The heavy reliance on the bonus payment as a means for collecting most of the economic rent associated with oil and gas leases can be seen in that, from 1953 through 1982, the federal government received $41.3 billion in bonus payments, $17.3 billion in royalty payments, and $302 million in rental payments for the 4,777 OCS tracts leased (see Figure 3–1).[1]

Critics of the cash bonus bidding system were successful in convincing Congress that the large, unconditional front-end payment required under this system leads to anticompetitive results and to sales of public resources at less than fair market value. As noted in Chapter 1, the OCS Lands Act Amendments of 1978 require that a minimum of 20 percent and a maximum of 60 percent of the total area offered for leasing each year in the five years following the passage of the act must be based on leasing systems other than conventional cash bonus bidding.[2] This legislation expired in 1983, leaving the Department of the Interior free to choose between bonus and royalty bidding systems.

---

1. U.S. Department of the Interior, Mineral Management Service, *Federal Offshore Statistics*, Dec. 1983, pp. 13, 64.

2. PL 95-372, sec. 205.

Figure 3–1. Government OCS Income by Source. Total 1953–1982 $58.9 Billion

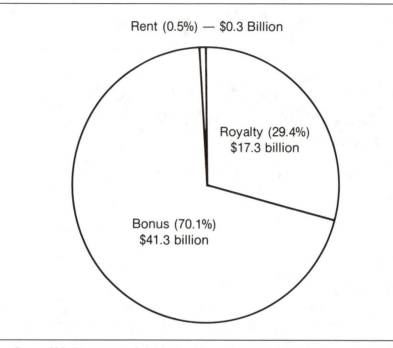

Rent (0.5%) — $0.3 Billion

Royalty (29.4%)
$17.3 billion

Bonus (70.1%)
$41.3 billion

Source: U.S. Department of the Interior, Minerals Management Service, *Federal Offshore Statistics,* Dec. 1983.

The various alternative bid variables will be analyzed in this and the following chapter. In this chapter we explore theoretically and empirically the efficacy of bonus bidding as a method of issuing offshore leases. In Chapter 4 we will analyze other alternative leasing systems authorized in response to the OCS Lands Act Amendments of 1978.

PERFORMANCE OF THE CASH BONUS BIDDING SYSTEM

The performance of the cash bonus bidding system can be analyzed in a number of ways. One method of analysis is based upon the application of economic theory to the behavior of firms acting under bonus bidding. The predictions of economic theory provide the first test of the efficacy of bonus bidding as compared to other methods of leasing. But performance cannot be tested in theoretical terms alone. A second method of analysis examines the historical record of offshore leasing. We have completed such a historical analysis, the results of which are discussed extensively below.

Bonus Bidding Promotes Resource Conservation

One desirable characteristic of a leasing system is that it should promote the conservation of resources, as described in Chapter 2. Conservation, or economic efficiency, has two aspects: The perceived benefits of any economic activity undertaken should be no less than the value of the resources employed, and the activity should be timed so that its present value is maximized. By eliminating activities whose costs are not justified by their benefits and by optimally timing activities that are economically beneficial, the expected net present value (or economic rent) of an oil and gas lease is maximized.

Perhaps the most desirable characteristic of bonus bidding is that it promotes resource conservation. Although considered costs by individual firms, the payments made by lessees to the government for the right to develop offshore properties are in fact "transfer payments." They are not true economic costs because they involve no use of economic resources; they merely redistribute income (economic rent) from the private to the public sector. Ideally, these payments should not affect the lessee's operating decisions.

Bonus bidding earns high marks in this area because the entire payment from lessee to lessor is made at the time the lease is issued. Thus, it does not affect subsequent marginal operating decisions. A course of action that maximizes the value of the lease to the lessee is, under these circumstances, identical to that which maximizes its social value, provided that there are no externalities, competition is effective, and the private discount rate is equal to the social discount rate. As we shall see in Chapter 4, some of the alternative leasing systems mandated by Congress do not promote economic efficiency in this way.

Bonus Bidding Identifies the Most Efficient Producer

Another desirable characteristic of a leasing system is that it grants each lease to the bidder who places the highest value on the resource. If the leasing method fails to do this, the winning bidder may fail to make the most efficient operating decisions, and conservation will not be served. Because bonus payments are made when the lease is awarded to the winning bidder, all competing bids are stated in terms of the perceived value of the lease at the time of the auction. The firm that values the lease most highly—and thus believes it can manage the lease most efficiently—is likely to bid the highest amount and win the lease. This is not true of other leasing systems. For example, royalty and profit share leasing can lead to ambiguity with regard to the true high bidder (see Chapter 4).

Bonus Bidding Minimizes Administrative and Compliance Costs

Still another desirable characteristic of a leasing method is that, other things being equal, it should minimize administrative and compliance costs. While all leasing methods require some administrative and compliance costs, methods that do not minimize government administrative costs will dissipate revenues collected from OCS leases. Unnecessary compliance costs lower lease values and reduce economic rent collection by the government.

The administrative costs of *pure* bonus bidding are small relative to other leasing systems because the entire rent transfer is in bonus form and is paid to the government at the time that the lease is issued. No expensive monitoring and policing is required, as is the case in royalty and profit share leasing. Similarly, lessee compliance costs are minimized. No outside party (except for the Internal Revenue Service) has a claim on any portion of the net or gross revenue from the lease. The lessee, therefore, need not be prepared for arguments over the soundness of his operating decisions.

A recent study by the U.S. General Accounting Office (GAO) is in general agreement with our assessment of administrative and compliance costs of bonus bidding relative to other leasing systems. While acknowledging that administrative and compliance cost data are lacking, the GAO concluded that these costs are likely to be greater if the net profit-share variable is used.[3] It also suggested that these costs would be similar for the various royalty leasing systems and the traditional system, cash bonus bidding with a fixed one-sixth royalty.[4] This result is not inconsistent with our analysis above, which relates to the administrative and compliance costs of a *pure* cash bonus bidding system (with no fixed royalty).

---

3. Report by the Comptroller General of the United States, *Congress Should Extend Mandate to Experiment with Alternative Bidding Systems in Leasing Offshore Lands*, GAO/RCED-83-139, 27 May 1983, p. 48.
    4. Ibid.

Bonus Bidding Facilitates Collection of Economic Rent

A bidding system should enable the government to collect the full economic rent associated with public lands. This implies that the lessee firms should be allowed a normal, competitive rate of return on their investments but that any surplus value (the economic rent) should be collected by the government. In order to assure that the public receives "fair market value," the leasing system should foster competition by allowing for ease of entry and exit of prospective lessees. Ease of entry facilitates competition, which in turn tends to promote the capture of economic rent by the public.

One of the principal criticisms of the bonus bidding system relates to its alleged inability to collect the full economic rent. However, this is fundamentally an empirical issue that can be addressed by means of available evidence. In the sections below, we review this evidence and the analyses that lead us to conclude that the bonus bidding system has very effectively transferred economic rent to the federal government.

REVIEW OF STUDIES OF LEASE PROFITABILITY AND TRANSFER OF ECONOMIC RENT

Economic theory suggests that if competition is effective, bonus bidding will allow the lessee to earn a normal rate of return on his investment with all economic rent being paid to the government. Our empirical study uses two types of economic analysis to determine overall profitability levels for our sample of OCS leases: internal rate of return analysis and regression analysis.

Internal Rate of Return Analysis

In this approach, a rate of return (yield on investment) is computed for all leases in the base period and for subcategories of leases. Internal rate of return (IRR) analysis is roughly comparable to discounted cash flow analysis, except that the purpose is to determine the *rate of return* earned on investment. In discounted cash flow analysis, an interest rate (or opportunity cost of capital) is specified in the model, and profitability is given in terms of the present value of the investment.

The IRR is defined as the rate of discount, i, which makes the present value of the stream of net revenue (or gross revenue (Rt) minus costs (Ct) and taxes (Tt) for each year) equal to zero. Algebraically:

$$0 = \sum_{t=1}^{n} \frac{Rt - Ct - Tt}{(1 + i)^t}$$

where n is the number of years until the project is abandoned.

The estimated IRR can be compared to rates of return earned on alternative (non-OCS) investments. A computed IRR much higher than the rates of return on alternative investments would indicate that bonus bidding produces anticompetitive results and that lessees are not returning the full economic rent to the government. A computed IRR approximately equal to rates of return available elsewhere in the economy would be an indication of competitive performance.

Multiple Regression Analysis

This approach estimates the parameters of a linear equation that explains the variation in a dependent variable by means of variations in several independent variables. The purpose of regression analysis in this context is to focus on economic variables that have a significant impact on winning bids in bonus bidding auctions. For example, we determine to what extent the high bid for individual leases is affected by (1) the number of bidders, (2) the economic size class of the winning bidder, (3) whether the winning bid was submitted jointly or by a single bidder, and (4) the actual value of recorded oil and gas production from each lease.

IRR and regression analysis differ in two important respects. First, regression analysis uses a set of proxy variables to represent the expected value of a lease at the time of the auction. IRR analysis, on the other hand, takes the high bid as given and, along with actual and estimated data, computes a rate of return for each lease category. Regression analysis can test for the statistical significance of the variables affecting the winning bid, but no similar test of the significance of variables affecting IRR can be made, since only one IRR observation is available for each lease category. In most cases, IRR analysis and regression analysis lead to the same conclusions; for simplicity of presentation, however, we have stated our IRR results first and our regression results thereafter. Where appropriate, we have attempted to point out any contradictions between the results.

Sources of Data

In both the IRR analysis and the regression analysis we have used the U.S. Geological Survey's Lease Production and Revenue (LPR) data bases.

This record includes names of winning bidders, high bonus bids, annual production by petroleum product through 1979, annual rental payments, annual royalty payments, and the total number of wells drilled on each tract by depth and spud-date through 1979. Our sample consists of the first 1,223 OCS leases issued in the Gulf of Mexico from 1954 through 1969. All sales involved a bonus bid with a fixed royalty at 16⅔ percent of product wellhead values. We have cut off our sample of lease sales at 1969 since at least a ten-year record is required to establish the full production potential of a lease. While a detailed explanation of the algorithms used in estimating costs and revenues is found in the Appendix, a brief explanation of the cost, revenue, and tax algorithms is given below.

Cost Data. Computation of the IRR is based on both known and estimated costs and revenues. On the cost side, exact data are available on all bonus payments, royalties, and rent payments from 1954 through 1969. We have estimated presale exploration costs and postsale exploration, drilling, development, production, interest, and abandonment costs. Based on the 1979 record of producing leases and using an exponential decline rate of 0.15 (equivalent to an annual 13.9 percent decline rate) for production, we have estimated production quantities and costs through the point of shutdown, assumed to be the year in which the after-tax net present value from each lease is maximized, or 2010 (whichever is earlier). An estimated abandonment cost is applied in the shutdown year. All past and future costs and product prices are in nominal terms.

Revenue Data.   On the revenue side, exact data are available on lease-specific production and revenue through 1979. A commercial crude oil price forecast by Data Resources, Inc., was the basis of our oil price assumptions through the year 2010.[5]

The predicted price of natural gas fully reflects the provisions of the Natural Gas Policy Act of 1978. This legislation calls for permanent price control over "old gas," which includes all gas produced from the leases in our sample.

---

5. Data Resources, Inc., 1981, pp. 175–78. The DRI forecast through the year 1995 anticipated a nominal compound annual price increase of 11.27 percent. Using the DRI-estimated rate of increase for the year 1995, we projected this series through the year 2010 to obtain a 10.66 percent compound annual crude oil price increase in nominal terms from 1981 through 2010. Given the decline in inflation rates and the decline in real crude oil prices that occurred between 1981 and the date of this writing (1984), it is apparent that the DRI nominal price forecast was incorrectly high for these years. Whether the forecast will remain incorrect through 1995 is still uncertain.

Tax Data.   The estimates of taxes attributable to each lease is based on actual and estimated cost and revenue streams. Oil industry profits are subject to ordinary corporate taxes plus a series of taxes unique to this industry. Our analysis considered the following thirteen tax provisions:

1. Corporate tax rates.
2. Corporate income tax surcharges.
3. Cost depletion.
4. Percentage depletion.
5. Expensing of intangible drilling costs.
6. Expensing of dry hole costs.
7. Depreciation of tangible drilling costs.
8. Windfall profits taxes.
9. Investment tax credits.
10. Capital gains taxes.
11. Minimum tax.
12. State income taxes (subject to the unitary tax formula).
13. State severance taxes.

A detailed explanation of the tax algorithms used in this analysis is also found in the Appendix.

Computational Results for Offshore Leases in the Aggregate

Table 3–1 provides data on rates of return for various aggregations of leases, together with other information. We find that on a before-tax basis, lessees earned a rate of return on equity of 13.16 percent on all 1,223 leases combined. The effect of a mixture of tax advantages enjoyed by the oil industry in the early period of our analysis, partially offset by the elimination of the percentage depletion allowance in 1975 and the imposition of the windfall profits tax in 1980, resulted in an after-tax rate of return only 2.42 percentage points lower, or 10.74 percent.

To complement the IRR analysis, we have also computed the average present value per lease. Table 3–1 shows that for all 1,223 leases, firms suffered an average present value loss of $192,128 per lease, using a 12.5 percent discount rate. By way of comparison, at a discount rate of 10 percent the 1,223 leases had an aggregate net present value of $115,575 per lease, while a 15 percent discount rate implies a loss per lease amounting to $334,893. Since all our costs and selling prices are in nominal dollars and our capital cost structure assumes some debt financing, we believe

Table 3-1. Economic Data for 1,223 OCS Oil and Gas Leases Issued in the Gulf of Mexico, 1954-1969.[a,b]

Aggregation Basis	Aggregate Internal Rate of Return		Average Present Value per Lease after Taxes (1954 Base Year) Using Alternative Discount Rates			Number of Leases Issued	Percent Dry Leases	Average Bonus per Lease	Undiscounted Average Gross Value of Production per Lease	
	Before Tax	After Tax	10%	12.5%	15%				Actual Through 1979	Estimated Through 2010
All 1,223 leases	13.16	10.74	$115,575	$-192,128	$-334,893	1,223.00	61.57	2,228,332	16,698,774	67,592,630
Big 8 firms	12.82	10.37	54,968	-221,873	-349,795	725.35	61.70	2,310,499	16,718,033	65,652,263
Big 9–20 firms	13.62	11.26	218,734	-150,770	-325,116	298.57	63.71	2,354,070	17,230,786	65,290,460
All other lessees	13.63	11.15	181,706	-145,763	-295,255	199.08	57.90	1,740,377	15,830,720	76,615,301
Solo bids	12.24	10.10	14,392	-228,436	-339,515	861.00	63.18	1,848,119	14,580,910	57,832,614
Joint bids	14.74	11.74	356,251	-105,761	-323,897	362.00	57.73	3,132,649	21,736,014	90,806,368
Wildcat leases	12.27	10.04	5,821	-249,045	-364,123	1,109.00	64.65	1,952,202	14,345,622	58,761,152
Drainage leases	18.27	14.59	1,183,260	361,594	-50,534	114.00	31.58	4,914,537	39,590,402	153,505,863
Number of bidders										
1	14.60	13.27	199,561	32,736	-53,397	411.00	74.21	469,522	7,981,616	29,739,722
2	14.40	12.55	233,598	3,067	-108,816	245.00	64.08	955,109	10,633,601	43,581,689
3 or 4	14.41	11.79	286,597	-78,060	-254,803	254.00	53.15	2,421,608	21,408,072	82,417,224
5 or more	11.99	9.32	-225,862	-732,747	-946,479	313.00	49.84	5,377,590	29,071,163	124,061,570
Bonus bid class										
$250,000 or less	14.34	12.91	146,057	13,942	-50,320	354.00	81.36	126,450	4,996,521	26,168,492
$250,001–$1,000,000	13.12	11.82	135,235	-35,715	-120,061	367.00	64.58	524,998	9,660,978	37,320,012
$1,000,001–$3,250,000	13.87	11.95	341,028	-68,953	-276,345	285.00	48.77	1,874,621	20,807,215	77,006,873
More than $3,250,000	12.52	9.41	-263,487	-954,594	-1,239,353	217.00	41.01	9,002,511	42,295,839	174,003,394

Source: W. J. Mead, A. Moseidjord, and P. E. Sorensen, "The Rate of Return Earned by Lessees Under Cash Bonus Bidding for OCS Oil and Gas Leases," *Energy Journal* 4 (no. 4, 1983):41.

[a]Where firms bid jointly, the bid shares have been attributed to each partner firm.

[b]The internal rate of return estimates reported here are not identical to those reported in Mead and Sorensen (1980) and Mead, Sorensen, Moseidjord, and Muraoka (1980) because of changes in algorithms and input data, most importantly higher forecasted oil prices and the calculation of IRRs based on the equity portion of investments in OCS leases rather than total invested capital.

that 12.5 percent is the appropriate discount rate. Using this discount rate, lessees suffered a loss averaging $192,128 per lease.

Comparing this rate of return to the average return on shareholder equity for all manufacturing corporations as reported by the Federal Trade Commission (FTC),[6] we find that the before-tax rate of return on the OCS leases was less than that for other industries (see Table 3–2).[7] Because the oil industry enjoyed net tax advantages relative to other industries over this period of time, the after-tax rate of return on the OCS leases is closer to the average after-tax return for all U.S. manufacturing industries. These tax advantages are primarily found in the percentage depletion allowance and the expensing of intangible drilling costs.[8] The close correspondence between after-tax rates of return for OCS lessees and for manufacturing industries generally implies that lessees have not been able to profit at the expense of the federal government by acquiring offshore leases at bargain prices. We find no support in the IRR analysis for the allegation that the government has received less than the full economic rent yielded by oil and gas leases sold under the cash bonus bidding system. The auction bidding process and level of competition produced outcomes consistent with the government's objective of receiving "fair market value."

These results appear surprising in view of the significant changes that occurred in energy prices and costs of production (including taxes) and in the legal, regulatory, and political environment of offshore leasing and the oil industry in the years following the issuance of these leases. It is likely that these changes were unanticipated at the time of the auctions, but the net effect was to generate economic outcomes consistent with competitive performance and bidders' expectations. These changes are discussed below.

Changes in Environmental Regulations. Since 1970, environmental regulations faced by the oil and gas industry, particularly with regard to offshore development, have become more stringent. This change can be traced back to the Santa Barbara oil spill of 1969. Following the spill, a

6. Federal Trade Commission, *Quarterly Financial Reports of Manufacturing Corporations,* various issues 1954 to 1978.

7. If the Data Resources, Inc., oil price forecast discussed above turns out to be erroneously high, then the actual internal rate of return will be even lower than we have estimated.

8. For a detailed discussion of these and other oil and gas industry tax provisions from 1954 through 1982, see Dennis D. Muraoka, "The Effect of Taxation on the Rate of Return on Outer Continental Shelf Leases Issued from 1954 to 1969" (unpublished doctoral dissertation, University of California at Santa Barbara, June 1981).

Table 3–2. Rate of Return on Stockholder's Equity for All Manufacturing Corporations, 1954–1983.

Year	Before-Tax Rate of Return	After-Tax Rate of Return
1954	18.5	9.9
1955	23.8	12.6
1956	22.6	12.3
1957	20.0	11.0
1958	15.4	8.6
1959	18.9	10.4
1960	16.7	9.2
1961	15.9	8.8
1962	17.6	9.8
1963	18.4	10.3
1964	19.8	11.6
1965	21.9	13.0
1966	22.5	13.5
1967	19.3	11.7
1968	20.8	12.1
1969	20.1	11.5
1970	15.7	9.3
1971	16.5	9.7
1972	18.4	10.6
1973	21.8	12.8
1974	23.4	14.9
1975	18.9	11.6
1976	22.7	14.0
1977	23.2	14.2
1978	24.5	15.0
1979	25.8	16.5
1980	21.9	13.9
1981	21.4	13.7
1982	14.1	9.3
1983	16.4	10.6
Average	19.9	11.7
Standard Deviation	3.0	2.0

Sources: Federal Trade Commission, Quarterly Financial Reports of Manufacturing Corporations, 1954 through 1982.

U. S. Department of Commerce, Bureau of Census, Quarterly Financial Report for Manufacturing, Mining and Trade Corporations, 1983.

moratorium on wildcat leasing was enforced to allow time for a review of the ecological impact of OCS oil and gas production. The moratorium was in effect until the December 1970 sale offshore from western Louisiana. The environmental review spawned new regulations that increased exploration and development costs, and consequently reduced the value of leases issued prior to 1970.

Changes in the Tax Treatment of Income From Oil and Gas.   Also in the 1970s, in part due to the political impact of the Santa Barbara spill and in part due to other political events, the tax treatment of income from oil and gas became less favorable. Tax legislation enacted in 1969 lowered the percentage depletion allowance from 27.5 percent to 22 percent of gross income, effective in 1970. The benefits of depletion were further reduced by the introduction of the minimum tax on preference income, which reduced the benefits of percentage depletion by an estimated 2 percent to 20 percent.[9] In 1975, the percentage depletion deduction was eliminated for all integrated companies, substantially increasing the tax liability of OCS firms. Finally, the Windfall Profits Tax of 1980 was enacted, recapturing from OCS lessees some of the revenue gains that were produced by higher crude oil prices.[10]

Changes in the Price and Cost of Crude Oil.   The price of crude oil is perhaps the most important determinant of the value of oil and gas leases. Throughout the 1950s and 1960s, the wellhead value of oil in the United States tended to increase modestly in nominal terms (1954 = $2.78 per barrel) and actually decreased in real terms. This real price decrease was reversed after 1972, when nominal crude oil prices increased sharply and unexpectedly, from $3.18 per barrel in 1970 to about $32 per barrel in 1981 (see Table 3–3). These price increases were probably the result of declining domestic production and the nationalization of Middle Eastern oil reserves. With the Arab-Israeli war of October 1973 and the Iranian

9. Gerard M. Brannon, "Existing Tax Differentials and Subsidies Relating to the Energy Industry," in G. M. Brannon, ed., *Studies in Energy Tax Policy* (Cambridge, Mass.: Ballinger Publishing Co., 1975), p. 5.

10. It might be argued that the relatively low after-tax IRR came about *only* because of the imposition of the windfall profits tax after the leases were issued. In order to test this hypothesis we reestimated the after-tax IRR in the absence of the windfall profits tax. The resulting after-tax IRR is 12.09 percent. Thus, even after the decontrol of crude oil prices, existing OCS leases earned after-tax returns comparable to manufacturing industries in general.

Table 3–3. Crude Oil and Natural Gas Prices and Costs From 1950.

	(1)	(2)	(3)	(4)	(5)
			Average	Average	
	Average	Average	Nominal	Real*	
	Nominal	Real*	Wellhead	Wellhead	Oilfield
	Wellhead	Wellhead	Price, U.S.	Price, U.S.	Machinery
	Price, U.S.	Price, U.S.	Interstate	Interstate	and Tools
	Crude Oil	Crude Oil	Natural Gas	Natural Gas	Price Index
Year	($/barrel)	($/barrel)	(cents/mcf)	(cents/mcf)	(1967=100)
1950	2.51	3.07	6.5	7.9	64.3
1955	2.77	3.15	10.4	11.8	79.7
1960	2.88	3.03	14.0	14.8	91.2
1965	2.86	2.96	15.6	16.1	95.2
1970	3.18	2.88	17.1	15.5	118.7
1971	3.39	2.98	18.2	16.0	122.6
1972	3.39	2.85	18.6	15.6	127.3
1973	3.89	2.89	21.6	16.0	133.2
1974	6.74	4.21	30.4	19.0	157.8
1975	7.56	4.32	44.5	25.4	196.3
1976	8.14	4.45	58.0	31.7	217.7
1977	8.57	4.41	79.0	40.7	236.6
1978	8.96	4.28	90.5	43.2	261.6
1979	12.51	5.31	117.8	50.0	289.6
1980	21.59	8.03	159.0	59.2	335.5
1981	31.77	10.83	198.0	67.5	401.0
1982	28.52	9.53	246.0	81.2	439.6
1983	26.19	8.64	262.0	87.5	427.0

*1967 dollars

SOURCES: W. J. Mead, et al., *Additional Studies of Competition and Performance in OCS Oil and Gas Sales, 1954–1975*, Final Report, USGS Contract No. 14-08-0001-18678, 30 Nov. 1980, p. 38.

Columns (1) and (3), U.S. Department of Energy, *Monthly Energy Review.*
Columns (2) and (4), American Petroleum Institute, *Petroleum Data Book.*
Columns (5) U.S. Department of Labor, Bureau of Labor Statistics, *Producer Price Index.*

revolution in 1978, followed by the Iran-Iraq war beginning in 1980, world oil prices escalated sharply.

These price increases would naturally have led to substantially higher values for existing oil and gas leases, but their effects were moderated by three contrary developments. First, on August 15, 1971, a wage and price freeze was imposed throughout the U.S. economy. The freeze was relaxed in three phases, eventually leaving only crude oil and petroleum products subject to controls. All OCS production from leases issued over the years 1954 through 1969 was classified as lower tier or "old oil" and was subject to the most restrictive price controls under the Energy Policy and Conservation Act of 1975. Second, although domestic oil prices were permitted to increase to some extent under controls, costs of exploring for and developing new oil supplies also increased. For example, the cost of oil field machinery and tools increased 327 percent from 1967 to 1983 (see Table 3–3). Finally, as a consequence of price controls, which established a multiple-tier system of prices, it became necessary for the government to develop methods to allocate low-priced crude and to equalize crude oil costs among refiners. These allocative and entitlements systems required expensive administrative bureaucracies both within the government and the affected firms. These additional private sector administrative costs reduced the value of existing OCS leases.

Changes in the Price of Natural Gas.   The attractiveness of natural gas increased markedly in the late 1970s, price controls notwithstanding. In the early years of OCS leasing, natural gas was not sought by bidders. Under price controls administered by the Federal Power Commission (FPC) after 1954, a relatively low natural gas price and the lack of gas transportation facilities often led to "flaring" when gas was discovered. By 1970, the infrastructure necessary to handle gas production was better established. But because gas production from the 1,223 leases in the sample was subjected to permanent price controls, the higher gas prices permitted for "new gas" under the Natural Gas Policy Act had little effect on the value of the leases.

Changes in the Worldwide Political and Economic Environment Affecting Oil and Gas Development.   After 1970, the political and economic stability of the Middle East gave way to periodic upheavals. The old concession system was replaced by nationalization. Control of oil and gas production was shifted from international oil companies to host countries. The individual countries have attempted, with mixed success, to coordinate their price and output decisions through two overlapping cartel organizations, the Organization of Petroleum Exporting Countries (OPEC) and the Organization of Arab Petroleum Exporting Countries (OAPEC). The most notable impact of this activity has been the sharp increase in the price of crude oil. This impact has been reinforced by the peaking of natural gas reserves (1970) and oil reserves (1967) in the United States. For both resources, declining reserves have led to declining production, forcing the United States to become more dependent on oil imports.

Sensitivity Analysis—Energy Prices and Production Decline Rates

Crude oil and natural gas prices for future years are subject to a high degree of uncertainty. For this reason we have prepared a sensitivity analysis on the after-tax IRRs based on future price scenarios 30 percent below and 30 percent above our standard scenario. Table 3-4 shows that even for these large variations in future prices, the effects on the estimated IRRs are not large. This is due to (1) the discounting process, (2) the expected decline in production over time, and (3) the fact that many of the leases were dry or unprofitable and were not producing beyond 1979 (see Table 3-5). In fact, only 357 leases (or 29.2 percent of the total number of leases in the sample) were producing beyond 1979. Table 3-4 also shows the sensitivity of the IRR to alternative production decline rates. The standard decline rate (a 15 percent exponential rate) was chosen on the basis of the actual decline rate for a sample of leases issued early in the leasing period. Again the range of IRR estimates is not large.

Table 3-4. Sensitivity of After-Tax Internal Rate of Return Estimates to Alternative Price Scenarios and Production Decline Rates.

		Estimated IRR (after tax)
Alternative price scenarios		
30% below standard scenario		9.74
15% below standard scenario		10.27
standard scenario		10.74
15% above standard scenario		11.16
30% above standard scenario		11.54
Alternative production decline rates		
Exponential	*Percentage Equivalent*	
0.10	9.05	12.20
0.15	13.93	10.74
0.20	18.13	9.65

Source: W. J. Mead, A. Moseidjord, and P. E. Sorensen, "The Rate of Return Earned by Lessees Under Cash Bonus Bidding for OCS Oil and Gas Leases," *Energy Journal* 4 (no. 4, 1983):44.

Table 3-5. The Record of Profitable, Productive but Unprofitable, and Dry Leases.

	Number	Percent	After Tax IRR
All Leases	1223	100.0	10.74
Profitable Leases*	267	21.8	18.74
Productive but unprofitable	199	16.3	negative
Dry Leases	757	61.9	negative

SOURCE: W. J. Mead, A. Moseidjord, and P. E. Sorensen, "The Rate of Return Earned by Lessees Under Cash Bonus Bidding for OCS Oil and Gas Leases," *Energy Journal* 4 (no. 4, 1983):43.

* Profitable leases are loosely defined as those having revenue greater than cost (positive present value at a zero discount rate).

Is Competition Effective?

In the previous sections we have shown that the after-tax rate of return earned on offshore oil and gas leases is consistent with effective competition, notwithstanding favorable and unfavorable changes in the industry. Furthermore, we have shown that this conclusion is not sensitive to changes in assumptions about future oil and gas price scenarios and production decline rates. Another measure of competitive performance in the lease sale market is the concentration ratio for the lease winners. Table 3-6 shows the number of leases acquired on a firm-by-firm basis over our study period. Before the 1984 mergers involving several large oil companies, the four largest buyers (Big 4) acquired 41.9 percent of the 1,223 leases, and the eight largest buyers (Big 8) accounted for 60.5 percent of the leases sold. These concentration ratios may be compared to averages for 314 U.S. manufacturing industries in 1972 computed by the FTC. The FTC found that the average Big 4 concentration ratio was 39.8 percent and the average Big 8 ratio was 52.6 percent.[11] Thus, concentration in the lease sale market is slightly higher than is characteristic of the economy in general. Most economists who specialize in industrial organization believe that the U.S. economy is effectively competitive.

Table 3-6 also shows how the Chevron-Gulf, Texaco-Getty, and Mobil-Superior mergers increase lease concentration ratios. Assuming that the

11. John E. Kwoka, Federal Trade Commission, Bureau of Economics, Working Paper Number 12, February 1978, Table 1, p. 6.

Table 3–6. Concentration Ratios in Gulf of Mexico OCS Lease Acquisition, 1954–1969, Before and After Getty, Gulf, and Superior Mergers.

	Before Mergers		After Mergers	
Company	No. of Leases Acquired	Percent	No. of Leases Acquired	Percent
Shell	165.00	13.49	165.00	13.49
Chevron	146.75	12.00	241.36	19.74
Exxon	106.57	8.71	106.57	8.71
Gulf	94.61	7.74	–	–
Texaco	69.50	5.68	102.10	8.35
Forest	57.00	4.66	57.00	4.66
Conoco	51.28	4.19	51.28	4.19
Sun	49.39	4.04	49.39	4.04
Std. Indiana	49.28	4.03	49.28	4.03
Mobil	46.95	3.84	67.94	5.56
ARCO	46.69	3.82	46.69	3.82
Union	44.96	3.68	44.96	3.68
Tenneco	42.48	3.47	42.48	3.47
Getty	32.60	2.67	–	–
Phillips	30.76	2.52	30.76	2.52
Cities	30.53	2.50	30.53	2.50
Placid	24.97	2.04	24.97	2.04
Superior	20.99	1.72	–	–
All other	112.69		112.69	
Total leases	1,223.00		1,223.00	
Big 4	512.93	41.94	615.03	50.29
Big 8	740.10	60.51	840.64	69.39

surviving firms would have acquired all of the leases won by the separate firms, concentration ratios would have increased to 50.28 percent for the Big 4 and 69.39 percent for the Big 8. While these postmerger ratios are above the averages, they still do not unequivocally indicate oligopsony power (market power among buyers of leases). An old rule of thumb advanced by Bain indicated that evidence of market power and monopoly profits begins when the Big 8 concentration ratio is larger than 70 percent.[12] More recent research has cast doubt on this rule and the consensus seems to be that monopoly power requires even higher concentration

12. Joe S. Bain, *Barriers to New Competition* (Cambridge: Harvard University Press, 1956), p. 195.

ratios and barriers to entry. One clear characteristic of the OCS oil and gas lease sale market is that barriers to entry are not high.[13] Anyone can enter this market as a bidder. Small firms are free to join with others and bid jointly. Wilcox has shown that in the twenty-year period from 1954 through 1973, 128 firms have won OCS leases.[14] This is a large number of competitors in itself, and it does not include other bidders and potential bidders who have not won leases. Nevertheless, one must conclude that the structure of the lease market is less competitive after the mergers of 1984 than before.

Trends in Rates of Return Over Time

The IRR record by lease sale is shown in Table 3–7 for wildcat and drainage lease sales separately. The low and negative rates of return of the initial five lease sales (from 10/13/54 through 8/11/59) appear to reflect excessive enthusiasm for the amount of oil likely to be found. The enthusiasm may have been the result of highly profitable offshore leases sold by the state of Louisiana from 1945 through 1948. We have explored this hypothesis by analyzing the profitability of these 271 Louisiana "Section 6 leases."[15] We found that on a before-tax basis, the IRR generated by the Section 6 leases was 18.98 percent. Available data do not permit us to calculate after-tax rates of return for the Section 6 leases, but we believe that these returns were viewed to be attractive from an oil industry perspective. Our view is based in part on the fact that the tax treatment of income derived from the production of oil was even more favorable in the years 1945 through 1948 than in later years. Bidders for the 1954 through 1959 leases might reasonably have expected to obtain similar results from their OCS leases, but (as our IRR results show) their expectations were not fulfilled.

Profitability Analysis of Subcategories of Leases

In the following sections, we analyze behavior and performance for subcategories of leases. Particular attention is paid to policy relevant

13. R. O. Jones, W. J. Mead, and P. E. Sorensen, "Free Entry into Crude Oil and Gas Production and Competition in the U.S. Oil Industry," *Natural Resources Journal* 18 (no. 4, Oct. 1978): 859–75. (This article also appears in *U.S. Energy Policy: Errors of the Past, Proposals for the Future.* See Selected Bibliography at the end of this book for publishing information.)

14. S. M. Wilcox, "Joint Venture Bidding and Entry in the Market for Offshore Petroleum Leases" (unpublished doctoral dissertation, University of California at Santa Barbara, March 1975), p. 92.

15. W. J. Mead, et al., *Competition and Performance in OCS Oil and Gas Lease Sales and Lease Development, 1954–1969,* USGS Contract No. 14-08-0001-16552, 1 March 1980, pp. 48–58.

Table 3-7. Internal Rate of Return by Lease Sale.

Lease Sale Date	Number of Leases Issued		After-Tax IRR (Percent)	
	Wildcat	*Drainage*	*Wildcat*	*Drainage*
10/13/54	90		7.73	
11/09/54	19		negative	
7/12/55	121		8.09	
5/26/59	23		negative	
8/11/59		19		7.38
2/24/60	147		13.98	
3/13/62	206		13.66	
3/16/62	205		11.01	
10/09/62		9		12.37
4/28/64		23		19.04
3/29/66		17		19.68
10/18/66	12	12	negative	14.16
6/13/67	158		9.77	
5/21/68	110		negative	
11/19/68	1	15	negative	16.54
1/14/69	10	10	7.65	13.93
12/16/69	7	9	4.35	26.05
Total, by class	1109	114	10.04	14.59
Total, all leases	1223		10.74	

SOURCE: W. J. Mead, A. Moseidjord, and P. E. Sorensen, "The Rate of Return Earned by Lessees Under Cash Bonus Bidding for OCS Oil and Gas Leases," *Energy Journal* 4 (no. 4, 1983):45.

variables including the following: (1) the size of the winning bid, (2) winning bid type (whether solo or joint), (3) lease type (whether wildcat or drainage), and (4) the number of competing bids submitted for the lease. In order to perform this analysis, regression techniques are used. The regression model is based on the economic theory of competitive bidding, which is reviewed in the next section. This will be followed by operational definitions of theoretically important variables as well as policy relevant variables. Finally, we will use the results from the regression analysis, along with additional IRR analysis, to address important issues relative to the effectiveness of alternative offshore leasing methods.

Theory of Competitive Bidding. An extensive literature exists concerning the decision-making behavior of bidders in auctions where the value of the object of the auction is not known precisely and where bidders realize their mutual interdependence.[16] The objective of each bidder is to choose a bid that maximizes his utility. In these models, the optimum bid is most often a function of the value estimate obtained, the level of uncertainty with regard to the lease value, and the number and bidding strategies of competitors.

The interaction of several bidders at the lease auction establishes the high bid, *Bmax,* which is of primary interest here. Theoretical bidding models, which assume that the bidders are identical in all respects, imply that *Bmax* is positively related to the expected value of the lease and the number of bidders, and inversely related to the amount of uncertainty regarding its value. In the limit, as the number of bids becomes large, *Bmax* tends toward the true value of the lease.[17]

Bidders in OCS lease auctions differ in size, experience in OCS lease operations, bidding form (whether solo or joint), and in the amount and quality of information they have at the time of the auction. These differences can be expected to lead to differences in bidding strategies and thus have an impact on the high bid. In particular, bidding models that assume asymmetrical distribution of information among bidders lead to the conclusion that the bidder in possession of superior information should bid more aggressively (a higher fraction of his value estimate) than his less informed competitors.[18] Our regression model formulations are designed to take into account the most conspicuous cases of bidder asymmetry in lease auctions.

The general formula of our high bid regression model is as follows:

$$Bmax = f(V,C,I,D)$$

where the independent variables are arrays that characterize certain features of the lease auction:

- V is composed of variables to capture the expected value of the lease,

- C is composed of variables that characterize the competitive structure for the lease,

16. See R. Engelbrect-Wiggans, "Auctions and Bidding Models: A Survey," *Management Science* 26 (Feb. 1980): 119–42.

17. See D. K. Reece, "Competitive Bidding for Offshore Petroleum Resources," *Bell Journal of Economics* 9 (no. 2, Autumn 1979): 169–84; see also, R. B. Wilson, "A Bidding Model of Perfect Competition," *Review of Economic Studies* 44 (1977): 511.

18. See E. L. Dougherty and M. Nozaki, "Determining Optimum Bid Fraction," *Journal of Petroleum Technology* 27, (1975): 349–56.

- *I* is composed of variables that characterize the amount and distribution of information available to bidders, and

- *D* is a set of dummy variables to correct for the pooling of time series and cross section data.

Regression Model Variables: Definitions and Hypotheses. The dependent variable in our regression models is the natural logarithm of the high bid. The independent variables are as follows:

1. The natural logarithm of the present value of production (LNPVP). Firms engage in presale geophysical and geological activities because exploratory information has positive value in identifying and evaluating productive tracts. Although presale tract evaluations are subject to a high degree of uncertainty, we advance a rationality hypothesis to the effect that a positive correlation exists between what firms think a tract is worth (based upon presale exploration) and the ultimate production from the tract. Since we believe that tracts with more promising geology are, in fact, more productive on average than other tracts, the record of production value for each tract can serve as a proxy for the perceived value of the tract at the time of the lease sale. For each lease, twenty-six years of production are included in the present value measure. Thus, leases issued in 1954 will have the entire period of historical production (through 1979) included, while leases issued in subsequent lease sales will have historical and forecasted values of production included, but only through year twenty-six following the lease sale. The discount rate used to compute present values is 10 percent, a rate we believe to be representative of that used by the oil industry for investment decision-making in the period of these lease sales.[19]

2. The natural logarithm of the number of wells drilled within twenty-four months (LNWELLS24). We have used present value of production from each lease as a proxy for the perceived quality of the lease at the time of the lease sale. But since over 60 percent of the leases in this study were dry (see Table 3–5), additional variables are needed to further differentiate among leases with respect to perceived quality. One of these is the log of the number of wells drilled within the first twenty-four months following the lease sale. It seems reasonable to assume that firms having an inventory of leases awaiting development would drill first on the most

19. The 10 percent discount rate was chosen to reflect the opportunity cost of *total* invested capital. A higher rate, 12.5 percent, was applied in an earlier present-value analysis because the concern there was with the rate of return to equity capital.

promising tracts. This assumption is consistent with profit maximization under capacity constraints, which requires that lower-cost resources be developed prior to higher-cost resources in order to preserve the intertemporal equality of the discounted value of the marginal benefit yielded by each unit of resources through the date of exhaustion.

Thus we expect a positive relationship between the number of wells drilled on each tract within a short time period after the lease sale and the high bidder's presale expectations concerning the quality of the tract. We have used a twenty-four-month period after lease sale as the time period for this variable because we believe most wells drilled during this period would be exploratory wells rather than productive wells.

3.   The natural logarithm of the number of acres (LNACRES). In making presale evaluations, firms analyze the geology of each tract to determine the nature and extent of possible hydrocarbon-bearing rock. For a geological structure of a given thickness, the amount of recoverable hydrocarbons will increase with the horizontal extent of the structure. Each increase in the surface area of the tract (or acreage) increases the size of the probable reserves that the tract may provide access to. Thus the tract size variable is designed to complement LNPVP and LNWELLS24 in capturing resource expectations and should have a positive impact on the size of the high bid.

4.   The natural logarithm of water depth (LNWATDEP). The value assigned by firms to tracts being considered for bidding is negatively correlated with the anticipated costs of developing the tract. Costs of well drilling and platform construction are the most important costs associated with tract development. These costs rose throughout the period of the study. Cost differences among different lease sale years are captured in the "year of sale" variable employed below. Cost differences between tracts leased in a given sale are most likely associated with differences in the water depth of the tracts. Deeper water means more costly wells and platforms. Greater water depth is also generally associated with greater distance from shore, which implies more costly transportation of workers and materials, and longer pipeline distances. Thus, as water depth increases, the relative cost of developing a tract should increase, and it is expected that the high bid will be less, *ceteris paribus,* for any given lease.

5.   The natural logarithm of the number of bids (LNNBIDS). Theoretical bidding models have the normative implication that the bid level for a particular bidder should be a decreasing function of the expected number of bidders. A recent empirical study by Gilley and Karels supports this theoretical proposition.[20] Despite this evidence, the high bid in these models is an increasing function of the number of bidders. Thus, at a theoretical level, the effect on the high bid of an additional bidder more than makes up for the reduction in each bidder's bid level. The variable LNNBIDS is interpreted to be an index of the intensity of competition for the lease, which is also related to the perceived value of the lease. We expect a positive sign.

   6. *Firm size of winning bidder—whether Big 8 or non–Big 8 (BIG801).* The firm size variable (Big 8 vs. non–Big 8) is included in the regression equation to test two alternative hypotheses concerning the effect of firm size on high bid. Firms were ranked based on worldwide sales in 1969 (see Table 3–8). The variable BIG801 has the value one if a winning solo bidder was a Big 8 firm or if any of the participants in a joint winning bid was a Big 8 firm, and zero otherwise.

   A thesis frequently advanced by critics of the bonus bidding system suggests that large firms exercise market power in the OCS lease market

---

Table 3–8. The 20 Largest U.S. Oil Companies, Ranked by Worldwide Sales, 1969.

Big 8	*Big 9–20*
1. Exxon	9. Tenneco
2. Mobil	10. Continental
3. Texaco	11. Phillips
4. Gulf	12. Occidental
5. Standard Oil of California	13. Sun
6. Shell	14. Union
7. Standard Oil of Indiana	15. Cities
8. Arco	16. Signal
	17. Standard Oil of Ohio
	18. Ashland
	19. Getty
	20. Marathon

Source: W. J. Mead, et. al., *Competition and Performance in OCS Oil and Gas Lease Sales and Development, 1954–1969,* USGS Contract No. 14-08-0001-16552, March 1, 1980.

---

20. O. W. Gilley and G. V. Karels, "The Competitive Effect in Bonus Bidding: New Evidence," *Bell Journal of Economics* 12 (Autumn 1981): 637–48.

and therefore pay less than other firms for leases of similar perceived quality. Alternatively, a second hypothesis says that large firms have advantages—in terms of borrowing capacity or ability to spread risk—which permit them to pay more for OCS leases, thus squeezing smaller firms out of this market.

In a competitive lease auction market, large firms could consistently outbid other firms and still earn a normal or higher rate of return on their OCS leases only if (1) imperfections in the capital market created a favorable differential in borrowing costs based on firm size, or (2) if such firms had special expertise—in some aspect of exploration or development of leases—that decreased their costs or increased the probability of finding oil and gas. However, our rate-of-return estimates for the leases analyzed here contradict the hypothesis that Big 8 firms perform better in OCS lease auctions than do smaller firms. Furthermore, the fact that smaller firms are able to participate in OCS lease investments through the vehicle of joint bidding, together with the practice within the oil industry of assigning the role of lease operator to that firm within the joint bidding combine having the greatest expertise in lease development, leads us to conclude that there is little likelihood that large firms could consistently outperform small firms in the market. Collusion among larger firms to rig the price at which leases are purchased from the federal government is also unlikely, since the number of firms participating in this market is large and growing and since there is no mechanism in a sealed bid auction to prevent firms that were not part of a collusive agreement from entering higher bids.[21,22] Support for this conclusion is given in the fact that in the entire period of OCS leasing (since 1954), there has never been one case of alleged bid-rigging. The most likely hypothesis concerning the effect of firm size on high bid is that firm size is not a significant variable.

7. *Character of winning bid—whether joint or solo (JOINT01).* The practice of joint bidding by firms for OCS leases has been cited by oil industry critics as a conspicuous example of anticompetitive behavior within the industry, in this case sanctioned by the federal government. In 1975, critics of joint bidding were able to force the Department of Interior to ban joint bidding among the largest oil companies, a ban that was later

---

21. Under the massive lease sale program introduced by former Interior Secretary James Watt, the average number of bidders per tract receiving bids has declined sharply from 2.95 bidders per tract issued from 1954 through 4/12/83 to 1.62 bidders per tract issued from 4/26/83 through 8/24/83.

22. See S. M. Wilcox, *note* 14 above.

endorsed by Congress in the Energy Policy and Conservation Act.[23] However, the effect of joint bidding on the size of winning bids is not so easily determined as these critics have suggested. While it might appear that joint bidding facilitates coordination among firms and thus reduces the number of bids for each lease, it is also true that joint bidding permits smaller firms to enter the OCS lease market and to spread risk among a larger number of leases. Since joint bidding permits risk spreading and risk reduction, the aggregate size of bids made by firms could increase rather than decrease.

Studies of the effect of joint bidding on the average number of bids for OCS leases have indicated that the net effect of joint bidding is to increase the number of bids.[24] Since we believe that joint bidding is mainly a technique used by firms to spread risk associated with the purchase of the most expensive leases, we would put forth the following hypothesis: While joint bidding has a small but positive effect on the amount of winning bids, it has a more significant positive impact on the size of winning bids for the most expensive leases. The variable JOINT01 is set equal to one for a joint winning bid and zero otherwise.

  8. Access to Special Information (NBOR and NNBOR). Leases offered for sale on the OCS are of two types. Wildcat tracts are located in unexplored, undrilled areas. By definition, no well-drilling data exist that would indicate the potential productivity of wildcat tracts. A drainage lease, on the other hand, is located near a proven deposit. Consider the example of drainage leasing illustrated in Figure 3–2. Tract A was leased in an earlier sale and oil was discovered. Well-drilling data and, perhaps, production data exist that lead the companies with a property interest in Tract A (and the USGS) to believe that the proven deposit extends into the drainage tract now offered for lease, called Tract B.

  The state of knowledge regarding the geology underlying a drainage tract is not uniform among firms in the industry. More knowledge is possessed by firms that are lessees of adjacent tracts (neighbors) than is

---

23. PL 94-163, Dec. 1975.

24. See J. W. Markham, "The Competitive Effect of Joint Bidding by Oil Companies for Offshore Leases," in J. W. Markham and G. F. Papanek, eds., *Industrial Organization and Economic Development* (Boston: Houghton Mifflin Co., 1970), pp. 116–35; see also, E. L. Dougherty and J. Lohrenz, "Statistical Analysis for Solo and Joint Bids for Federal Offshore Oil and Gas Leases" (Paper presented at meeting of Society of Petroleum Engineers, Bakersfield, Calif., April 13–15, 1977).

Figure 3–2. Illustration of Drainage Tract Leasing.

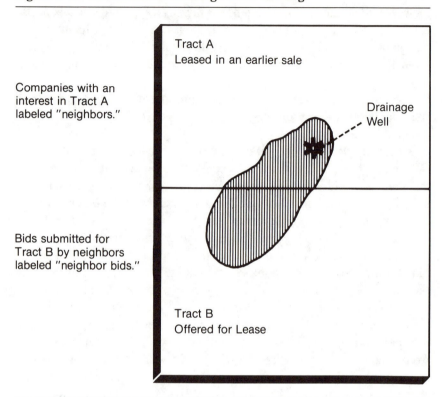

Companies with an
interest in Tract A
labeled "neighbors."

Tract A
Leased in an earlier sale

Drainage
Well

Bids submitted for
Tract B by neighbors
labeled "neighbor bids."

Tract B
Offered for Lease

possessed by firms in general. But even non-neighbor firms may be
presumed to know more about a drainage tract than is known by firms in
general about any given wildcat tract, since part of the geological
knowledge gained by neighbor firms in their exploratory activities on adjacent tracts is communicated to the industry by official and nonofficial
reports of lease activity.

Economic theory suggests that firms with superior information
(neighbors) would generally make higher bids for drainage tracts because
the discount factor for risk facing these firms would be lower than for
other firms. Theory also suggests that non-neighbor firms bidding on
drainage tracts would make higher bids, on average, than firms in general
would bid for wildcat tracts—because the average quality of drainage
leases is higher and because the degree of uncertainty facing firms bidding for drainage leases is lower.

To test these hypotheses, dummy variables are assigned to bidders for each lease. Using these dummy variables, winning bids for wildcat leases are distinguished from (1) winning non-neighbor bids for drainage leases; and then, separately, from (2) winning neighbor bids for drainage leases. We hypothesize that the correlation between high bid and both of these dummy variables should be positive, and that the estimated value of the coefficient for neighbor bids should be higher than for non-neighbor bids.

9. *Percentage share of past leases won (PSHPASTL).* An important factor affecting the pattern of bidding for leases is the experience of the bidder in prior lease sales in the Gulf of Mexico. Firms that have been high bidders for acreage leased in prior lease sales would most likely have a better knowledge of the underlying geology of the Gulf of Mexico and of the expected competition among bidders than firms with less experience in bidding and exploring. Under this interpretation, accumulated experience is an asset to a bidder. Less experienced bidders have to "pay a fee," partly in the form of higher bids, in order to acquire this asset. Furthermore, if the early experience in bidding for OCS leases was disappointing, firms with a larger share of winning bids in prior lease sales would be most likely to correct for this experience in framing their current bids. If, on the other hand, early sales on the OCS had produced high profits for firms, the most experienced firms would make proportionately higher bids for current OCS leases. Our study of rates of return earned by firms that were winning bidders in the early lease sales (especially 1954–1959, see Table 3–7) on the OCS shows that these rates of return were below normal. Thus, we hypothesize that firms with a larger percentage share of past leases issued in the Gulf of Mexico would make lower (winning) bids for leases in current lease sales. The correlation between the variable percentage share of the past leases (PSHPASTL) and the high bid should be negative over the sample period.

Results of Regression Analysis. The results of the regression model are shown in Table 3–9, Results of Regression Analysis. All of the explanatory variables in this model are significant at the 5 percent level, with the exception of the variable representing bid type (JOINT01). The results indicate that joint bidders paid neither significantly more nor significantly less than solo bidders for leases in our sample. The other independent variables performed according to theoretical expectations, with the exception of the variable relating to firm size (BIG801). We now combine this analysis with additional IRR analysis to answer some important policy issues regarding the efficacy of bonus bidding.

Table 3–9. Results of Regression Analysis (dependent variable: the natural logarithm of high bid).

Variable	Parameter Estimate	T-Ratio[*]
INTERCEPT	6.711	12.80
LNPVP	0.009	2.11
LNWELLS24	0.498	10.86
LNACRES	0.703	10.93
LNWATDEP	−0.096	−2.28
LNNBIDS	1.193	31.21
BIG801	0.276	3.47
JOINT01	−0.005	−0.07
NBOR	1.443	10.28
NNBOR	1.089	7.14
PSHPASTL	−0.039	−5.27
R-Square = .6587		

SOURCE: W. J. Mead, A. Moseidjord, and P. E. Sorensen, "Competition in OCS Oil and Gas Lease Auctions—A Statistical Analysis of Winning Bids," *Natural Resources Journal* (forthcoming, January 1986).

[*] All variables are significant at the 5 percent level (two-tailed test) except JOINT01.

The Impact of Firm Size—Do Large Oil Companies Have Monopsony Power in the Oil and Gas Lease Market? The variable BIG801 has a positive and significant sign. Thus Big 8 firms tend to submit higher bids than smaller firms in our sample. It can be shown, however, that this applies to one special case only. Winning bids submitted for wildcat leases by Big 8 solo bidders are significantly higher than for wildcat leases won by non–Big 8 solo bidders. We interpret this to mean that the larger firms are better able to carry the high risk of bidding alone in areas where no drilling information is available prior to sale. This finding is consistent with that reported by Millsaps and Ott based on ten lease sales in 1972–1975.[25] However, smaller firms bid as aggressively as larger firms for such high risk acreage when they bid jointly, indicating that the joint bid option is used by smaller firms for risk spreading.

The economic performance (IRR) by firm size shows no clear pattern (see Table 3–1). The after-tax IRR is highest for the intermediate sized

25. S. W. Millsaps and M. Ott, "Information and Bidding Behavior by Major Oil Companies for Outer Continental Shelf Leases: Is the Joint Bidding Ban Justified?" *Energy Journal* 2 (no. 3, July 1981): 71–90.

firms (11.26 percent), followed by the smallest firms (11.15 percent), with the Big 8 firms having the lowest return (10.37 percent). The computational results do not support the hypothesis that Big 8 firms have an "unfair advantage" in the lease markets. Smaller firms compete successfully for leases and earn slightly higher returns. The federal government actually captures a larger share of the economic rent from leases won by Big 8 firms than from leases won by smaller firms. This indicates that a policy of granting smaller firms advantages in competing for OCS leases will be at the expense of collecting a lower share of economic rent.

Does Joint Bidding Reflect Anticompetitive Behavior?   The average high bid for leases won by joint bids is much higher than for solo bids, $3.1 million vs. $1.8 million (see Table 3–1). The nonsignificance of the variable JOINT01 in the regression model indicates that this difference is due to factors other than the bidding arrangement. In particular, Table 3–1 shows that the leases won by joint bids are generally of better quality (as judged by the percentage of dry leases and by the undiscounted average gross value of production per lease) than those won by solo bids.

Joint bidding allows for both risk spreading and information pooling. The former suggests that leases won by joint bids should command a lower IRR than leases won by solo bids; the latter, that jointly owned leases should realize a higher rate of return. Our analysis indicates that the latter tendency is strongest. Joint winning bids earned an IRR of 11.74 percent compared to 10.10 percent for solo winning bids. Further evidence of the advantages of information pooling can be found in the fact that for the most risky leases (wildcat leases), the return to joint bids was 11.12 percent, while the comparable return to solo bids was 9.38 percent. For drainage leases, the return was almost unaffected by the bid type: 14.46 percent for solo and 14.74 for joint bids. This pattern does not support the hypothesis emphasizing anticompetitive effects of joint bidding since it is hard to understand why such anticompetitive effects would be observed only for wildcat leases and not for drainage leases. Furthermore, the after-tax IRR from jointly owned leases (11.74 percent) is approximately the same as the return on equity in manufacturing industries over the period 1954–1969 (11.7 percent).

In summary, joint winning bids are higher than solo winning bids because the pooling of information by the joint bid participants enables them to identify the high quality tracts that warrant aggressive bidding. Nevertheless, we find that leases purchased jointly yield a higher rate of return to the lessees than do solo bid leases.

Returns on Wildcat Versus Drainage Leases.   The fact that a reservoir believed to extend into a drainage tract has been located prior to sale of the drainage tract makes drainage tracts more valuable than wildcat tracts. The frequency of nonproductive wildcat leases (64.5 percent) is more than twice that of drainage leases (31.58 percent). In terms of average undiscounted gross value of production, drainage leases are nearly three times as valuable as wildcat leases. The average high bid for a drainage tract ($4.9 million) is therefore much higher than for a wildcat tract ($2.0 million). The regression model shows that both bidder categories in drainage lease sales, NBOR and NNBOR, submit significantly higher bids for drainage leases than for the base-case wildcat leases. Furthermore, neighbor winning bids are, as expected, higher than non-neighbor winning bids. On average, the difference is nearly $2 million.

Lessees of the more valuable drainage leases also earn a higher after-tax IRR (14.59 percent) than do lessees of wildcat tracts (10.04 percent). Our explanation for this difference is the asymmetrical distribution of information in drainage lease auctions. Bidders in possession of superior information (neighbors) are better able to identify drainage tracts that show very promising geology and that actually turn out to be very productive. Although the winning bids for these tracts are very high, neighbors still earn a substantially higher after-tax IRR (16.42 percent) than do non-neighbors (12.49 percent). The benefits of superior information can also be seen in the fact that neighbors have a lower percentage of dry leases (26.98 percent) than non-neighbors (35.42 percent) and a much higher gross production value per lease. Non-neighbors realize a higher IRR than the aggregate for all wildcat leases (10.04 percent), most likely because they bid cautiously against better-informed neighbors to avoid winning drainage leases by overestimating lease values. This cautious bidding strategy gives good economic returns when a bid is successful in winning a lease. The observed outcome in drainage lease auctions is consistent with the theoretically expected outcomes in asymmetrical information bidding models, such as those of Wilson, and Dougherty and Nozaki.

The consequences of asymmetrical information for bidding outcomes lead to the following policy question: Should the information advantage of neighbors be eliminated by making exploratory data on drainage reservoirs available to all potential bidders prior to drainage leases? We have two reasons for advising against such a policy.

First, the possibility that a drainage reservoir may be located adjacent to any wildcat tract increases the expected value of wildcat tracts and thus the high bids for these tracts. This explains, at least in part, why wildcat leases yield relatively low returns to the lessee. The government should not be concerned with equalizing the bidding outcomes for wildcat and drainage leases separately. Rather, the concern should be with the aggregate rate of return for wildcat and drainage leases combined. As we have argued above, lessees did not earn excessive rates of return in the aggregate over the period we have studied.

Second, a lessee firm that locates a drainage reservoir generates an information externality for which it should be compensated. Rather than granting an explicit subsidy to such a firm and incurring the related administrative costs (as Stiglitz has suggested), the federal government can minimize costs by allowing the market to grant such firms an advantage in bidding for adjacent drainage tracts. This leads to efficient exploration of drilling prospects located close to lease borders and a higher amount of economic rent potentially available to the public.[26]

Does Increased Bidder Participation Lead to Higher Bonus Bids and Lower Returns? The natural logarithm of the number of bidders (LNNBIDS) has a positive and significant impact on the high bid in the regression model. From Table 3-1, it is evident that higher-quality leases attract more bidders. The percentage of dry leases decreases and production value increases as more bids are submitted for a lease. Part of the increase in the average bonus bid in Table 3-1 is most likely explained by the correlation between the number of bidders and the perceived value of a lease. But the number of bids also has a strong and independent competitive effect on the high bid. This effect causes the after-tax IRR to decline monotonically from a maximum of 13.27 percent for one-bidder leases to a minimum of 9.32 percent for leases receiving five or more bids, as shown in Figure 3-3.

One possible explanation for the reduction in the after-tax rate of return as the number of bidders increases is a phenomenon called the "winner's curse."[27] Given the uncertainty of offshore oil and gas leases, the winners at the auctions may be the firms who most overvalue the leases. If this

26. See E. Miller, "Some Implications of Land Ownership Patterns for Petroleum Policy," *Land Economics* 49 (Nov. 1973): 414–23; see also, F. M. Peterson, "Two Externalities in Petroleum Exploration," and J. E. Stiglitz, "The Efficiency of Market Prices in Long Run Allocations in the Oil Industry," both in G. M. Brannon, ed., *Studies in Energy Tax Policy* (Cambridge, Mass.: Ballinger Publishing Co., 1975), pp. 101–13 and 55–98, respectively.

27. E. C. Capen, R. V. Clapp, and W. M. Campbell, "Competitive Bidding in High Risk Situations," *Journal of Petroleum Technology* 23: 641–53.

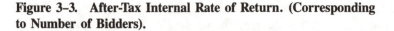

Figure 3–3.   After-Tax Internal Rate of Return. (Corresponding to Number of Bidders).

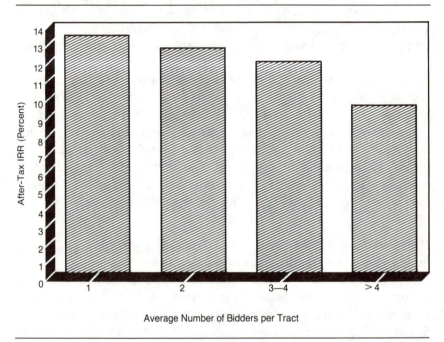

Average Number of Bidders per Tract

SOURCE: W. J. Mead, et al., *Additional Studies of Competition and Performance in OCS Oil and Gas Sales*, 1954–1975, USGS Contract No. 14-08-0001-18678, 30 Nov. 1980.

is true, it is likely that winning bidders will ultimately earn a relatively low rate of return on their leases, unless they systematically adjust their bids downward. Logically this nonaggressive bidding behavior would become more pronounced the larger the number of bidders.[28] The fact that the after-tax internal rates of return are smaller the greater the number of bidders would indicate that this nonaggressive behavior is not apparent. This finding is consistent with the results of an empirical study by James L. Smith of OCS leases issued from 1974 through 1976. Smith concluded that "there is no evidence that the phenomenon of winner's curse is sufficiently important to lead to the adoption of nonaggressive bidding strategies."[29]

28. J. L. Smith, "Non-Aggressive Bidding Behavior and the 'Winner's Curse,'" *Economic Inquiry* 19 (July 1981): 380–88.
29. J. L. Smith, "Risk Aversion and Bidding Behavior for Offshore Petroleum Leases," *Journal of Industrial Economics* 30 (no. 3, March 1982): 251–69.

Although leases with a small number of bidders realize a relatively high rate of return, it does not follow that the government should choose to indiscriminately reject winning bids for leases with a small number of bidders (as has been suggested in a recent study by Ramsey[30]). The high rate of return to leases with a small number of bidders is outweighed by the low rate of return to leases receiving a large number of bidders. Any change in bid rejection policies would induce a change in bidding strategies, since lessees could no longer expect to be compensated for low returns on leases receiving many bids (where they may be subject to the "winner's curse") by winning leases yielding higher returns due to a small number of bids and thus a smaller bonus payment. Again the conclusion follows that the government should be concerned with economic rent capture in the aggregate. Given the IRR results reported earlier, restrictions on specific categories of leases are unnecessary.

In the regression model, the variable expressing the percentage share of past leases sold (PSHPASTL) is negative and significant, as expected. This supports the hypothesis that more experienced bidders tend to bid more cautiously as a result of the disappointing economic returns in early lease sales or, conversely, that inexperienced firms must be willing to pay an "entry fee" to gain experience in evaluating OCS resources.

Does Bidding Appear to Be Rational?   Our findings lend support to the argument that bonus bidding for oil and gas leases is rational. Measuring lease quality by either ex-post data on percent dry holes or the actual average gross value of production through 1979, we find a close correlation between the value of production and the value of bonus bids. This conclusion is supported by the regression model, which indicated a high degree of consistency with hypotheses derived from economic theory.

Bonus Bidding and Optimal Risk Sharing[31]

The ideal leasing system should optimally allocate the risk of OCS oil and gas leasing between the lessee and the lessor.[32] If the federal government

---

30. J. B. Ramsey, *Bidding and Oil Leases,* Contemporary Studies in Economic and Financial Analysis, vol. 25 (Greenwich, Conn.: FAI Press, 1980).

31. This section is based on Asbjorn Moseidjord and Dennis D. Muraoka, "Managing the Risk of Outer Continental Shelf Oil and Gas Leases," in M. H. Hamza, ed., *Proceedings of the IASTED International Symposium on Energy, Power and Environmental Systems, San Francisco, June 4–6, 1984* (Anaheim, Calif.: Acta Press, 1984).

32. Hayne L. Leland, "Optimal Risk Sharing and the Leasing of Natural Resources, with Applications to Oil and Gas Leasing on the OCS," *Quarterly Journal of Economics* 92 (Aug. 1978): 413–37.

is more risk-neutral than the private sector lessees, the government should bear the bulk of the uncertainty of OCS activities. If risk-averse private firms must bear all of the uncertainty of offshore oil and gas development, they will discount their bid levels and underinvest in their OCS operations. One of the primary criticisms of the bonus bidding system of leasing is that it shifts all the uncertainty of offshore production to the lessee firms. This may appear to be a very serious defect if each OCS lease is considered in isolation and the risk of the lease is measured as the standard deviation of its return (or some other measure of dispersion).

To illustrate this, consider the 1,223 Gulf of Mexico OCS leases discussed above. Of these, fully 757 or 61.9 percent were abandoned as dry leases, and another 199 or 16.3 percent were productive but unprofitable (see Table 3–5). The after-tax present value of the 1,223 leases varied from a low of −$41 million (a loss) to a high positive value of $117 million, with a standard deviation of $9.4 million. However, any conclusions regarding the uncertainty of these leases, based on the analysis of individual leases in isolation, are inappropriate, because participants in OCS lease auctions generally hold more than one lease at a time.

Financial investment theory indicates that the proper measure of risk of an investment is its contribution to the uncertainty of the *total* portfolio of assets held by the investor. This will generally be less than the standard deviation of returns from the individual lease in isolation. Diversification of a portfolio can reduce uncertainty if the assets in the portfolio are not perfectly positively correlated.[33] The uncertainty that can be eliminated through diversification is commonly referred to as unsystematic or diversifiable risk. The remaining risk is referred to as systematic or nondiversifiable risk.

Risk-averse firms or individuals require a premium to accept nondiversifiable risk. Empirical work by Wagner and Lau has determined that about fifteen different stocks should be held in an investor's portfolio in an effort to fully eliminate unsystematic risk.[34] We have performed a similar analysis to illustrate the advantages of risk diversification for portfolios of OCS leases.

Using the data from the 1,223 leases described above, the real, after-tax present value as of the sale date was generated for each of the leases. The discount rate used was that which set the aggregate present value of

33. J. F. Weston and E. F. Brigham, *Managerial Finance*, 6th ed. (Hinsdale, Ill.: Dryden Press, 1978), pp. 249–82.

34. W. H. Wagner and S. C. Lau, "The Effect of Diversification on Risk," *Financial Analysts Journal* 27 (Nov.–Dec. 1971): 48–53.

the leases equal to zero. The risk properties of twenty-five different port-folio sizes were considered, the first portfolio having one lease, the sec-ond two leases, and so forth. In order to estimate the risk of a portfolio containing n leases ($n = 1, 2, 3, \ldots, 25$), 100 portfolios were selected at random from the set of 1,223 leases, each containing n leases. This ex-periment was performed using ex-post magnitudes as proxies for ex-ante magnitudes and is, therefore, based on price, cost, and the government regulatory regime that actually prevailed from 1954 to the present. The standard deviation of returns to these 100 portfolios was used as an estimate of the total risk of a portfolio containing n leases. These data were in turn fitted, using regression techniques. Division of the standard deviation by the number of leases in the portfolio yields the average stan-dard deviation per lease in the portfolio, or the average contribution of a lease to the total portfolio risk. More important, the marginal standard deviation per lease, or the additional contribution of a lease to the total portfolio risk, can be estimated by finding the increase in the standard deviation of the portfolio due to adding one more lease. These computa-tional results are shown in Figures 3–4 and 3–5.

Note that the marginal risk of a lease declines rapidly when it is added to a relatively small portfolio. With one lease, the marginal risk is $9.1 million, while the marginal risk of the fifth lease is only $2.3 million, and the marginal risk of the tenth lease is further reduced to $1.6 million. Beyond fifteen leases, the additional decline in marginal risk is relatively small. The importance of this finding is that a lessee does not have to be very large in terms of lease holdings in order to reap most of the benefits of risk diversification. The actual lease holdings of firms active on the OCS are shown in Table 3–10. The company ranked twentieth in terms of acres acquired in the Gulf of Mexico from 1954 through 1969 controlled 14.24 leases when all the fractional portions of leases are added together. A count of the fractional portions reveals that the twentieth firm held in-terests in twenty-four leases.

In fact, a risk-averse firm can take full advantage of portfolio diver-sification by consciously acquiring assets with a low correlation of returns, rather than selecting its portfolio at random, as was done here. This can be accomplished in part by giving careful consideration to the correlation coefficients of lease returns when bidding at lease auctions (e.g., by selecting leases in differing geographical and geological areas), by trading in the postsale transfer (or assignment) market, or by entering joint ventures and farm-outs with other firms. Firms can further reduce uncertainty by acquiring onshore oil and gas properties or assets in entire-

Figure 3–4. Total Risk of a Portfolio of OCS Leases as a Function of the Number of Leases in the Portfolio.

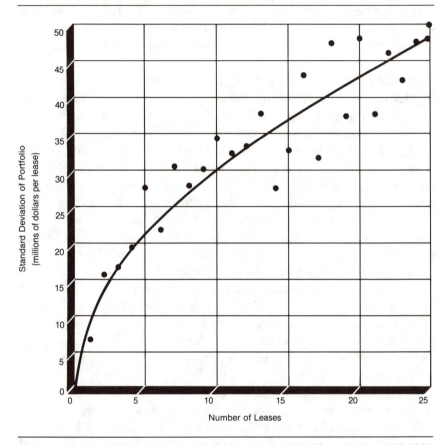

SOURCE: A. Moseidjord and D. D. Muraoka, "Managing the Risk of Outer Continental Shelf Oil and Gas Leases," in M. H. Hamza, ed., *Proceedings of the IASTED International Symposium on Energy, Power and Environmental Systems, San Francisco, June 4-6, 1984* (Anaheim, Calif.: Acta Press, 1984), pp. 9-11.

ly different industries. Many OCS lessees have already done this. Additionally, while this discussion has focused on the diversification of risk within a given time period, firms can also diversify risk across time periods.

The preceding analysis considered the ways in which a risk-averse firm can diversify the riskiness of offshore leases. Another important question is, To what extent are OCS lessees risk averse? The greater the aversion to risk, the greater the premium that is necessary to undertake nondiver-

Figure 3–5. Marginal Risk of a Portfolio of OCS Leases as a Function of the Number of Leases in the Portfolio.

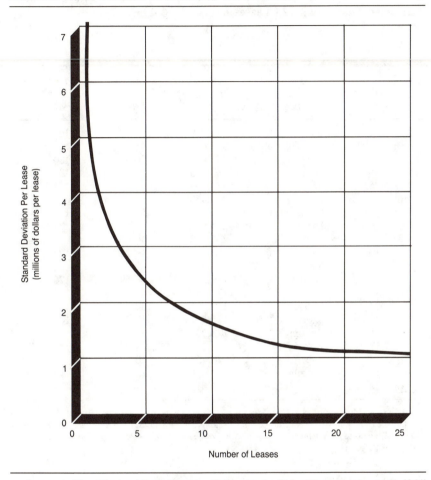

SOURCE: A. Moseidjord and D. D. Muraoka, "Managing the Risk of Outer Continental Shelf Oil and Gas Leases," in M. H. Hamza, ed., *Proceedings of the IASTED International Symposium on Energy, Power and Environment Systems, San Francisco, June 4-6, 1984* (Anaheim, Calif.: Acta Press, 1984), pp. 9-11.

sifiable risks. James Smith has found that the majority of firms in the industry exhibit significant risk aversion, but the degree of risk aversion decreases with firm size.[35] In fact Smith concludes that seven major companies (Exxon, Texaco, Mobil, Standard of California, Gulf, Stan-

35. J. L. Smith, *note* 29 above.

Table 3-10. Leasing Results for the 20 Largest Firms by Acreage: Attributed Shares of 1,223 Leases Issued, 1954–1969.

Rank by Acreage	Company	Acres Leased Through 1969	Number of Leases Acquired Through 1969	Number of Lease Interests Acquired Through 1969
1	Shell	754,110	165.00	167
2	Std. Oil Cal.	575,685	146.75	165
3	Exxon	481,448	106.57	120
4	Gulf	430,883	94.61	132
5	Texaco	324,806	69.50	101
6	Forest	269,453	57.00	57
7	Continental	213,416	51.28	122
8	Union	204,523	44.96	73
9	Mobil	204,418	46.95	78
10	Std. Oil Ind.	203,629	49.28	82
11	Sun	202,103	49.39	66
12	Arco	199,209	46.69	126
13	Tenneco	179,530	42.48	49
14	Getty	130,596	32.60	105
15	Cities	125,597	30.53	104
16	Phillips	122,230	30.76	37
17	Placid	87,187	24.97	35
18	Superior	70,454	20.99	27
19	Murphy	60,036	12.50	13
20	Kerr-McGee	54,511	14.24	24

SOURCE: A. Moseidjord and D. D. Muraoka, "Managing the Risk of Outer Continental Shelf Oil and Gas Leases," in M. H. Hamza, ed., *Proceedings of the IASTED International Symposium on Energy, Power and Environmental Systems, San Francisco, June 4–6, 1984* (Anaheim, Calif.: Acta Press, 1984), p. 10.

dard of Indiana, and Shell) "can reasonably be said [to] have attained risk neutrality."[36]

SUMMARY OF ANALYSIS OF BONUS BIDDING

The system used for leasing oil and gas resources on public lands should be consistent with (1) maximizing the economic rent inherent in these resources, (2) collecting the full economic rent, (3) identifying the most

36. Ibid.

efficient producer, (4) optimally allocating the risk of offshore development between the private and public sectors, and (5) minimizing administrative and compliance costs. The traditional method of leasing offshore lands for oil and gas production has been bonus bidding with a one-sixth royalty. Recently this method of leasing has come under attack for allegedly not returning the fair market value of OCS resources to the government. In this chapter we have analyzed the efficacy of the traditional cash bonus bidding system in terms of economic theory and by examining the actual record of federal offshore leasing in the Gulf of Mexico.

Our analysis indicates that bonus bidding promotes economic efficiency in that it does not affect marginal decision-making of lessee firms. Because the entire payment for the lease is made at the time the lease is issued, administrative and compliance costs are minimized. Furthermore, bonus bidding tends to identify and award the lease to the most efficient firm.

The empirical analysis of the first 1,223 Gulf of Mexico OCS leases strongly supports the hypothesis that competition has been effective in transferring the full economic rent to the government. Further analysis of the leasing record shows that (1) big firms have no "unfair" advantage over small firms, (2) joint bidding is an effective means for risk spreading and information pooling and has no anticompetitive implications, (3) owners of adjacent tracts have a significant information advantage when bidding for drainage leases (and this leads to superior economic returns), and (4) the larger the number of bidders, the higher the winning bid and the lower the lessee's rate of return.

We also conducted a multiple regression analysis of high bids, which showed the bidding process to be economically rational. By several measures of lease quality, high bids were observed to rise as lease quality rose, while high bids fell as potential costs of development increased, *ceteris paribus.*

Bonus bidding places the bulk of the uncertainty of offshore development on the lessee firms. However, the uncertainty of offshore leasing should not be measured in terms of the uncertainty of individual leases in isolation, but rather in terms of the contribution of an individual lease to the uncertainty of a portfolio of leases. While offshore leasing is a risky business, the uncertainty of offshore leasing is overstated when it is not examined in the context of portfolio theory.

Our analysis concludes that the bonus bidding system has highly desirable theoretical advantages that are complemented by the competitive performance demonstrated in our empirical studies. In the next chapter, we examine the major alternative OCS leasing systems in an attempt to determine whether they offer any advantages relative to the traditional method of leasing.

4

AN ECONOMIC ANALYSIS OF ALTERNATIVE BID VARIABLES

In the previous chapter we examined the OCS bonus bidding record in terms of economic efficiency (resource conservation). In this chapter we analyze several alternative leasing systems that have been authorized for use by the Department of Interior. Specifically, we evaluate royalty, profit share, and work commitment bidding.[1]

ROYALTY BIDDING

Under royalty bidding some of the problems associated with bonus bidding are eliminated, although new problems are introduced. Contestants are asked to make their offers in terms of a percentage of gross wellhead value payable to the government for each barrel of oil or thousand cubic feet of gas produced from the lease. Royalty bidding has three major advantages.

The Advantages of Royalty Leasing

First, payments to the government correspond with production, both in amount and timing. If a lease is found to be dry, then no payments are made. If a lease is highly productive, then payments are correspondingly large. Under royalty leasing, the political embarrassment of a small fee

---

1. These leasing systems were previously summarized in Table 1–2.

being paid to the government for a large find is avoided.

Second, because there is no fixed bonus, no "front-end" payment is required. This may stimulate additional bidding competition, particularly from smaller firms without as much access to capital markets. Firms are able to obtain leases with no payment being made to the government prior to production from such leases.

Third, the requirement of the contingency royalty payment rather than a lease bonus shifts some of the uncertainty of oil and gas development back to the lessor from the lessee. Because this uncertainty is shifted, a risk-averse lessee will require a smaller risk premium and will bid more for the tract.

The Disadvantages of Royalty Leasing

While royalty bid leasing solves some of the problems of bonus bidding, there are substantial disadvantages arising out of a royalty bidding system that do not exist in the bonus bidding system.

Royalty Leasing May Not Identify the Most Efficient Firm.   An effective sale procedure must identify and grant the lease to the firm that will maximize its present value. Royalty leasing does not necessarily reveal the true "high bidder' (and hence the most efficient firm) among the competitors for a lease tract. This occurs because competing firms submit bids as rates and are not required to reveal their production plans and cost functions. In contrast, bonus bids implicitly reveal the bidder's expected revenue flow and cost schedule. To illustrate this problem consider the following hypothetical example.

Two firms are formulating bids on a royalty bid sale. Firm A expects to receive $9.5 million in gross revenue from the tract entirely during the fifth year after the sale date. For this expected revenue it bids a 50.5 percent royalty, which would be payable as production proceeds in five years. Firm B anticipates $9 million in revenue from the tract; however, its production will occur four years from the sale date. Firm B bids a 50 percent royalty for the right to develop the tract. On the basis of the two royalty bids, Firm A would be awarded the tract. However, if the present value of the revenue derived from the two bids is considered, the rankings could be reversed. For example, at a 10 percent discount rate the present value of Firm A's bid is $2.98 million while the present value of Firm B's bid is $3.07 million.

Royalty Leasing Leads to Premature Abandonment. Royalty bidding (and royalty payments) lead to premature abandonment of leases. The problem is illustrated in Figure 4–1. Costs of production are low in the initial phase of reservoir life. As production proceeds, reservoir pressure declines and production costs per barrel increase. In the absence of a royalty charge, and assuming a constant price of crude oil (currently approximately \$30 per barrel), total production would equal q_1. Beyond that point, the cost of producing an additional unit of output is higher than its value. With total production q_1, the value of the resources used to produce the last barrel of oil are exactly offset by the value of the oil produced. Social waste results from production either beyond, or short of, this point.

Figure 4–1. Illustration of Premature Abandonment as a Result of Royalty Leasing.

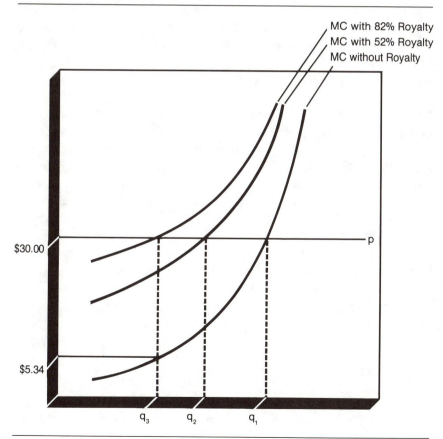

If the required royalty was 52 percent, production would be terminated at output, q_2. With an 82 percent royalty, the property would be abandoned at q_3, when operating costs rise to $5.34 per barrel and the royalty equals $24.66 per barrel (.822 x $30).[2] But from the viewpoint of conservation, production should be continued until economic costs rise to $30 per barrel. Thus a royalty leads to premature abandonment of a lease and loss of valuable resources. It is correct to describe this as "premature abandonment" because the royalty payments are merely transfers of economic rent from the operator to the government. They are not true economic costs in the sense that labor and materials are economic costs.

Premature abandonment might be avoided by successive reduction of royalty rates to zero. Everyone gains from reducing royalties to zero, relative to fixed royalties. Profits to the operator would increase, additional royalties would accrue to the government, employment would be higher, and the nation would receive additional oil production at social costs below the cost of imported oil. Under the 1953 OCS Lands Act, the Interior Secretary was granted the authority to reduce royalty rates.[3] Possibly because of the administrative difficulty and political vulnerability, this authority has never been exercised.

Sliding Scale Royalty Leasing—Secondary and Tertiary Recovery of Resources Is Discouraged. The 1978 amendments explicitly provide for a sliding royalty scale.[4] A sliding scale royalty differs from a fixed royalty in that the royalty rate increases or decreases with the quarterly value of production. As a consequence, larger discoveries result in larger royalty rates. The Interior Department is currently using six different sliding scale formulas. Summary information regarding the six sliding scale formulas is found in Table 4-1. Actual royalty rates as a function of quarterly production value are shown in Figure 4-2. Despite the sliding scale, inefficiencies and consequent losses in economic rent would still result. Investments in secondary or tertiary recovery would still be retarded. Such investments cause output, and therefore royalty payments, to increase.

While costs would rise, these increased costs are ignored by a royalty system based on *gross* income only. The net effect is to depress the return on investments. In cases where the return on investment of secondary and

2. These royalty rates correspond to the lowest (51.8 percent) and highest (82.2 percent) winning bids on eight royalty bid leases issued in an experimental OCS lease sale in October 1974.

3. 43 U.S.C. 1334(a)(1). These provisions are retained in the 1978 amendments. See 43 U.S.C.A. 1334 (Supp. 1979).

4. 43 U.S.C.A. 1337(a)(1)(C) (Supp. 1979).

Table 4–1. Sliding Scale Royalty Rates.

	Minimum Royalty Rate	Quarterly Production Value at Which the Royalty Rate Begins to Increase	Maximum Royalty Rate	Quarterly Production Value at Which the Royalty Rate Tops Out
	(percent)	*($ million)*	*(percent)*	*($ million)*
Formula 1	16⅔	1.50	50	34.83
Formula 2	16⅔	13.24	65	1,662.85
Formula 3	16⅔	15.93	65	3,423.82
Formula 4	16⅔	10.81	65	445.24
Formula 5	16⅔	22.30	65	4,793.35
Formula 6	16⅔	14.79	65	1,197.21

SOURCE: U. S. General Accounting Office, Comptroller General's Report to Congress, *Congress Should Extend Mandate to Experiment With Alternative Bidding Systems in Leasing Offshore Lands*, GAO/RCED-83-139, 27 May 1983.

Figure 4–2. Sliding Scale Royalty as a Function of Quarterly Production Value.

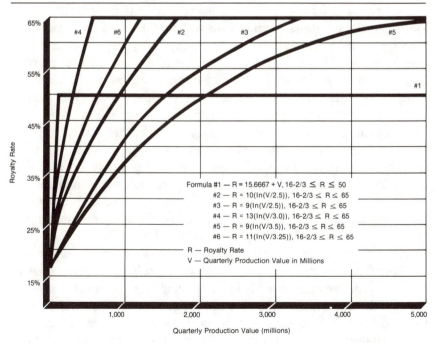

Formula #1 — $R = 15.6667 + V$, $16\text{-}2/3 \leq R \leq 50$
#2 — $R = 10(\ln(V/2.5))$, $16\text{-}2/3 \leq R \leq 65$
#3 — $R = 9(\ln(V/2.5))$, $16\text{-}2/3 \leq R \leq 65$
#4 — $R = 13(\ln(V/3.0))$, $16\text{-}2/3 \leq R \leq 65$
#5 — $R = 9(\ln(V/3.5))$, $16\text{-}2/3 \leq R \leq 65$
#6 — $R = 11(\ln(V/3.25))$, $16\text{-}2/3 \leq R \leq 65$

R — Royalty Rate
V — Quarterly Production Value in Millions

tertiary recovery projects is shifted from attractive to unattractive, the government suffers a loss of economic rent, and society suffers the penalty of resource misallocation (the conservation objective is not served).

Furthermore, additional administrative costs are incurred. With royalty rates determined solely as a function of production, the operator has an incentive to reduce production below the most efficient rate that would maximize economic rent. But production rates should be set at levels that maximize economic efficiency, not at rates that are influenced by a royalty payment schedule. Government administrators may try to avoid these problems with careful surveillance of the operator, but this requires expensive administration.

It should also be noted as a drawback of royalty bidding that some smaller fields, which could be profitable to operate under low or zero royalty rates, become submarginal with higher royalty rates. Thus, a newly discovered small field would be termed uneconomic to operate and would not be developed at all. The result is a monetary loss to the government and a social loss to the entire nation.

Royalty Leasing Adversely Affects Production Timing.   Royalty bidding not only leads to premature abandonment or possible nondevelopment of a property, it also adversely affects timing of production. Other things being equal, the profit-maximizing firm will first develop those resources with the lowest production costs. By putting off the higher costs to the future, the firm minimizes the present value of the total costs of production. Royalty payments are treated by firms as marginal production costs (even though such costs are actually transfer payments). The firm is therefore induced to defer production beyond the date that would have been chosen in the absence of the royalty payment. Of course, the problem of deferral of production can be remedied by imposing diligence requirements on lessee firms. Current OCS leasing policy imposes two diligence requirements. First, firms are required to make nominal rental payments on all acreage until production begins; and second, if production does not begin during the term of the lease (usually five years), the lease reverts to the federal government. But, it is difficult to construct diligence requirements that will induce firms to adjust production to the ideal production profile of a property. It is extremely unlikely that the two diligence requirements currently in force would have this effect. And even if theoretically workable diligence requirements could be developed, in practice this would require costly monitoring and enforcement on the part of government. Such monitoring would add still another layer of the administrative (and compliance) costs that reduce the yield of economic rent (for more analysis of diligence requirements, see Chapter 5).

The combined effect of royalty payments on the total amount and timing of production is illustrated in Figure 4–3, which shows the production over time of a hypothetical property both with and without a royalty payment. The area under each curve represents the total production from the property. Note that the total area under Curve *A* (representing production without a royalty) exceeds that of Curve *B* (representing production with a royalty). This illustrates the "premature abandonment" aspect of royalty leasing. Also note that production under Curve *B* occurs later in time than Curve *A*. This illustrates the delaying effect, discussed above, that royalties have on production.

Royalty Leasing Encourages Speculation. Royalty leasing can lead to undesirable speculation in offshore leases. It is perhaps easiest to see this point if offshore leases are viewed as options contracts. When a lease is granted by the federal government, the lessee firm acquires an option to produce the oil and gas that may be discovered on the tract. The option expires if production does not begin during the term of the lease (usually

Figure 4–3. Royalty Leasing and Production Timing.

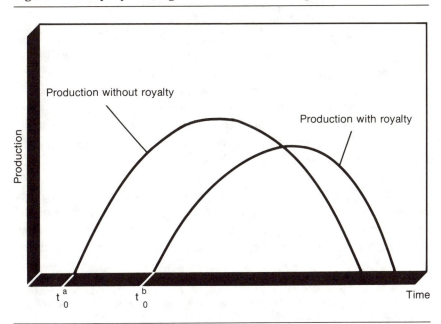

Production without royalty

Production with royalty

Production

t_0^a t_0^b Time

five years). It is valid regardless of the future price of oil and gas or future changes in technology or in regulatory policies.

Options play an important role in a market economy in that they allow economic agents to adjust their asset portfolios to a desired level of risk. The owner of an asset can increase the income that will be generated by his portfolio with certainty by selling an option that allows the buyer to purchase the asset for a limited period of time at a predetermined price, called the *strike price*. Speculators are on the opposite side of this transaction. They buy the option, and profit if the market price of the asset rises above the striking price during the time period that the option contract is in effect. If the price of the asset should fail to rise above the strike price during the prescribed time period, the speculator loses his investment (the money that was paid for the option). In effect, the owner of the asset accepts the payment from the speculator (called the *option premium*) in return for giving up the possibility of added financial gains if the asset price increases above the strike price. Options of this sort are referred to as *call options*. Options and speculation provide a valuable economic function by allowing the reallocation of risk.[5]

In the absence of a fixed bonus, royalty leasing allows lessees to acquire lease options at no cost. Lessees can, therefore, submit very high bids in order to win the leases while having no real intention of developing the leases unless the price of oil or gas should jump dramatically (as it did in 1973–74 and 1979–80), or unless oil or gas is actually discovered on a nearby tract. If neither of these conditions occurs during the lease term, the lessee simply surrenders the lease to the federal government, having paid only the nominal annual rental payment (and perhaps a fixed bonus) for the option. Furthermore, a provision in leasing legislation allows negotiations between the lessor and lessee to reduce the royalty percentage to a level that would permit profitable operation of the lease. Thus, even if the lease is eventually brought into production, the high royalty bid may be nullified and the *actual* lease price determined by negotiation.

While the government has little experience with royalty leasing (see below), it has a longstanding policy of selling timber from the national forests using a "royaltylike" bid variable called a *log-scale bid*. A log-scale bid represents the amount that a firm is willing to pay per thousand

---

5. For a more detailed discussion of offshore lease agreements as option contracts, see G. G. Pickett, *An Option Valuation Model of Bonus Bidding and Profit-Share Bidding for Offshore Oil and Gas Leases* (unpublished doctoral dissertation, University of California at Santa Barbara, 1983).

board feet for any timber removed from the tract. Historically, the actual payment for the timber has been made at the time of harvest. But in the case of timber sales, firms that fail to satisfy their contractual obligations are subject to penalties. Nevertheless, the U.S. government has been plagued with a rash of speculative bidding that has caused firms to seek government "bailouts" from unprofitable contracts.[6] Clearly, the incentive for speculative bidding in OCS royalty lease sales is even higher, as the limited empirical evidence suggests.

Empirical Evidence From Royalty Lease Sales

Our theoretical analysis of the problems inherent in royalty payments is generally supported by the limited experience of the federal government with leasing systems involving nontraditional royalty requirements. The first such experience involved lease sale 36, which was conducted by the Department of the Interior in October 1974 using the royalty rate as the bid variable. Ten tracts offshore from Louisiana were offered for lease in an experimental royalty bidding auction. Eight tracts were eventually leased at royalty rates ranging from 51.8 percent to 82.2 percent. In the three years following the sale, a very limited amount of drilling was carried out on the royalty tracts.[7] Firms that had contracted for high royalty requirements seemed to be waiting for evidence of production potential on nearby acreage before committing themselves to an expensive drilling program.

An analysis of this sale, conducted by the Interior Department, concluded that although the tracts leased under royalty bidding received more bids on average than tracts leased in the same sale under the conventional bonus bidding plus one-sixth royalty system, the high royalty rates created by competitive royalty bidding had seriously eroded the potential commercial value of the tracts. As a result of royalty bidding, according to this analysis, there was a high probability that "no royalties will be realized

6. Marilyn Chase, "Timber Firms Seek Bailout from the U.S.," *Wall Street Journal*, 1 April 1983, p. 15. For a more detailed analysis of the nature and problems of federal timber sale procedures, see Dennis D. Muraoka and Richard B. Watson, "Improving the Efficiency of Federal Timber Sale Procedures," *Natural Resources Journal* 23 (no. 4): 815–25; and Dennis D. Muraoka and Richard B. Watson, "Economic Issues in Federal Timber Sale Procedures," in R. T. Deacon and M. B. Johnson, eds., *Forestlands: Public and Private* (San Francisco: Pacific Institute for Public Policy Research, 1985).

7. Mike Long, "Royalty Bidding Experiment Turns Sour," *Oil and Gas Journal* 75 (no. 18, May 1977): 132.

at all—in fact government receipts on the tract could be negative due to tax write-offs."[8] The Interior Department's analysis concluded that (1) royalty bidding tracts have a high probability of yielding no commercial finds, and (2) ultimate recovery from any commercial find will be low.[9] Furthermore, the high winning bids for tracts thought to be of low potential value confirm that speculation under a no-cost option system would be a problem with royalty leasing.[10]

A second experiment with royalty bidding on OCS oil and gas leases occurred in the Lower Cook Inlet OCS lease sale of October 27, 1977. For this sale, the Interior Department designated forty-six of the 135 tracts offered as royalty bid tracts, with fixed bonus requirements ranging from $142,848 to $3,416,832. The thirty tracts leased under the royalty bidding system showed no apparent difference in the number of bidders per tract (3.53) as compared to bonus bid tracts leased in the same sale (3.50). An analysis by the Department of the Interior concluded that the cost to the government of using royalty instead of cash bonus bidding in this sale was between $26 million and $78 million—losses in net rents and in royalties on lost production that would have been developed under the conventional bonus bidding system.[11]

The passage of the OCS Lands Act Amendments in 1978 required the Department of the Interior to use nontraditional leasing methods for between 20 and 60 percent of all leases offered for sale over a five-year trial period ending in 1983. Over that time, the Interior Department did not deviate from the cash bonus as the bid variable; however, it did use forms of royalty payments other than the traditional 16⅔ percent. The fixed royalty rates used were 12½ and 33⅓ percent. In addition, six different sliding scale royalty formulas were used (see Table 4–1). While the production record from the leases issued using these alternative royalty formulations is too short to undertake a full analysis of their effectiveness, a preliminary analysis can be performed on the effect of these alternative royalty rate structures on the level of bonus bids and the level of competition.

One of the criticisms of the traditional cash bonus bid with one-sixth

8. Department of the Interior, Office of the OCS Program Coordination, "An Analysis of the Royalty Bidding Experiment in OCS Sale #36," 1975.

9. Ibid.

10. Ibid.

11. Department of the Interior, Office of Policy Analysis, "Royalty Bidding in OCS Lease Sales," memorandum to Assistant Secretary, Policy, Budget and Administration, 1977, p. 4.

royalty leasing system is that the large bonus bid may serve as a barrier to entry to the offshore lease market. By increasing the royalty rate, it is expected that firms will adjust their bonus bids downward on two counts. First, assuming that the production profile of the lease would be identical to that attained using the traditional leasing system, if higher royalty payments are made during the productive life of the lease, then the level of the bonus bid should be adjusted downward if firms are to maintain the same level of profit. However, as noted earlier, royalty payments alter the productive profile of a lease. They tend to slow the rate of production and reduce total production (see *"Royalty Leasing Adversely Affects Production Timing,"* above). The total effect is to reduce the present value of a lease. By reducing the present value of a lease, one should also expect lower bonus bids.

The General Accounting Office (GAO) has undertaken a study of the impact of alternative royalty rate structures on the level of competition (as measured by the number of companies participating in the auction and the number of bids submitted), while correcting for differences in the perceived value of a tract. Their results indicate that when the royalty rate is the bid variable, there are significantly more bids and greater participation by small companies in OCS lease auctions. The use of the one-third fixed royalty also significantly increased the number of bids and led to greater participation at the auction by both small and large companies.

The results of the GAO analysis of sliding scale royalty sales were mixed. For three of the six sliding scale formulas, the number of bids and level of participation were *not* found to be statistically different from those attained by the traditional leasing system. Two of the sliding scale formulas (formulas 4 and 6) tended to significantly increase the number of bids and the level of participation, while one formula (formula 1) significantly *reduced* the participation of companies in general and small companies in particular. The smaller fixed royalty rate had the anticipated effect of reducing the participation of small firms, but did not significantly affect the total number of bids submitted.

The effect of alternative royalty payments on the level of bonus bids was mixed in the GAO study. Neither the lower one-eighth fixed royalty or the larger one-third fixed royalty had a statistically significant impact on the level of bonus bids. Four of the six sliding scale formulas (formulas 1, 2, 3, and 5) also failed to have a statistically significant impact on bonus bids. As noted above, sliding scale formulas 4 and 6 increased the level of competition, but they had opposite effects on the level of bonus bids.

Formula 4 significantly increased the level of bonus bids, while formula 6 significantly decreased the bonus bid level.[12]

In summary, royalty leasing has the advantages of eliminating the front-end payment and shifting some of the uncertainty of offshore leasing to the lessor. It has the further political advantage that the payments for offshore leases, on a lease-specific basis, are more closely aligned with the actual production from the lease. However, royalty leasing also has substantial disadvantages. First, royalty payments result in reduced efficiency and therefore reduced economic rents. This is due to the premature abandonment and mistiming of production that occurs under royalty leasing. The larger the royalty payments, the greater the loss in economic rent. Sliding scale royalty rates avoid the problem of premature abandonment if the rate is reduced to zero at the appropriate points in time. They still result in a slowing of production, however, and will artificially discourage investments in secondary and tertiary recovery; moreover, they result in wasteful administrative and compliance costs—all of which lower economic rents available to the government. Royalty leasing also obscures the true high bidder at lease auctions and can lead to undesirable speculation in bidding for offshore tracts.

PROFIT SHARE LEASING

Profit share leasing offers a popular alternative to bonus bidding and royalty leasing. Under profit share bidding, each bidder offers a percentage of the net profit on a lease as payment to the government for the right to explore and develop the lease. The profit share is applied only if profits are positive.

The Advantages of Profit Share Leasing

There are four possible advantages of profit share bidding. First, it is an improvement over royalty bidding in that the profit share is based on some definition of net income (profit) rather than gross income. This means that as a field approaches exhaustion, its profit declines toward zero. Unless the profit share bidding system also requires a fixed royalty payment, the problem of premature abandonment is avoided. This is illustrated in Figure 4–4. In the absence of profit share payments, the ap-

---

12. For a detailed discussion of the GAO regression model, see U.S. General Accounting Office, Report by the Comptroller General of the United States, *Congress Should Extend Mandate to Experiment With Alternative Bidding Systems in Leasing Offshore Lands*, GAO/RCED-83-139, 27 May 1983, "Appendix II, Econometric methods and results," pp. 62–66.

Figure 4–4. Profit-Share Leasing Does Not Induce Premature Abandonment (if Profit is Properly Defined).

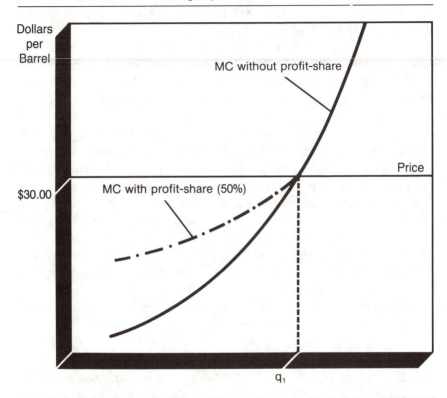

propriate production from the lease is q_1, where the marginal production cost is equal to the marginal revenue. Unlike royalty payments, which appear to the lessee as marginal production costs that are added to the other marginal costs shown in Figure 4–4, profit share payments are determined as a percentage of the difference between the marginal revenue and marginal cost. Thus, as marginal cost converges on marginal revenue at higher levels of production, the amount of the profit share payments also declines, reaching zero at output q_1. Marginal decision-making is thus unaffected by the profit share payments, and total production is unchanged (provided that profit is defined appropriately; see *"The Problems of Defining Profit,"* below).

Second, profit share bidding avoids the front-end loading problem that is characteristic of bonus bidding (unless profit share bidding is paired with a fixed bonus requirement). No payments are due until production appears and profits accrue to the operator. In the absence of these front-end payments, smaller and less well financed operators may enter the bidding competition and possibly win leases.

Third, payments correspond with benefits. Dry holes require no profit share payment. Conversely, the occasional rich discovery producing high profit requires larger payments to the government. This would avoid some of the political embarrassment associated with a Prudhoe Bay–size discovery.

Fourth, a pure profit share bidding agreement may constrain over-zealous regulators and environmentalists from imposing uneconomic costs on oil exploration and production. Under the profit share system, any economic waste is clearly shared by the operator and the government. It should be pointed out that when government imposes postbidding environmental or other costly regulations, the initial impact is on lessee profit. But rational bidders will quickly come to expect a repetition of such regulation in subsequent sales. These expectations will be factored into future bid calculations; thus, the cost of such regulations will ultimately be borne by the government. Where the government shares in all operating costs explicitly (as in the profit share system), excessive regulations should not be as easy to impose.

Profit Share Leasing and Uncertainty.   When the cash bonus bidding system is compared to the profit share system, it is frequently concluded that the latter is superior in terms of risk sharing. This follows when a profit share lease is compared to a cash bonus lease with joint bids not allowed. Thus the comparison is between a lease with two partners (the lessee and the federal government) and a lease held by a single firm. From the point of view of the lessee, the profit share lease has a dispersion of present value smaller than that for a comparable bonus lease. Both upside and downside risks are reduced. In this sense, profit sharing leads to risk sharing. The dispersion of present value to be realized by the lessee is reduced because the lessee holds a smaller economic interest in the venture. Under cash bonus bidding, bidders have the option of reducing the size of their economic interest by submitting joint bids. In our opinion, the correct comparison is, therefore, between net profit sharing and cash bonus bidding allowing for joint bids and joint ventures. In such a comparison, the profit share system is inferior for two reasons.

First, under the net profit-share system, the lessee and the lessor become partners in a joint venture. The government "contributes" part of the bid by accepting a smaller front-end payment (equal to zero under pure profit-share bidding) in return for a share of future net profits. In this limited sense, profit share leasing is analogous to joint bidding under the cash bonus system. The profit share is the federal government's share of a joint bid, negotiated at the time of the lease auction. However, this arrangement deprives the bidder of the option to negotiate a joint bid (a similar contract) with a partner of its own choice. Thus the profit share system is only a special case of cash bonus bidding, with one option removed. This limitation will make a lease less valuable to a bidder under profit share bidding than under cash bonus bidding.

Second, there are real world circumstances that cause the federal government to be an inferior joint venture partner (apart from the conflict between the role of lessor and joint venture partner). Under current profit-share rules, the federal government does not share exploration costs incurred on dry leases. This has the effect of increasing the downside risk relative to a comparable cash bonus, joint bid lease. Furthermore, the federal government, as a joint venture partner, is not able to contribute the same amount of technical and economic expertise to the venture as would a private partner. From this perspective, we conclude that the profit share system is inferior to the cash bonus system with joint bidding in terms of risk sharing.

The Disadvantages of Profit Share Leasing

There are substantial disadvantages associated with the profit share bidding system.

The Problems of Defining Profit.   While most people may consider computation of profit to be a simple and straightforward calculation, profit is actually difficult to define. For example: (1) The producer may be a vertically integrated company or be involved in trading of oil with another company. In either case, an arm's length sale of oil does not take place. "Revenue" becomes subject to estimation and requires administrative expense on the part of both the lessee and the lessor. (2) If a company wishes to do some research and development concerning oil exploration and production, it is likely to do so on leases involving profit share payments rather than on other company production utilizing bonus or royalty payments. (3) Where a company has a mixture of highly efficient and less efficient drilling rigs or ships, it is likely to use the poor equipment on the profit share lease and reserve the best equipment for other company operations. (4) When a company needs to train crews in drilling and reservoir development, it is likely to do its training on the profit share leases. (5) "Goldplating" (poor cost control) is likely to occur on profit share leases where the share paid to the government is very high and the retained share is low. Evidence of this practice may be found in the Long Beach (Wilmington) field, where profit shares paid to the government are extremely high. (6) Profit share leases may exhibit excessive public relations expenditures, particularly when such expenditures produce benefits for the lessee company as a whole. (7) In the event of a shortage in the supply of oil field equipment such as occurred in 1973 and 1974, available supplies are likely to be allocated by lessees to non-profit-share leases first.

As noted earlier, one problem with the current profit share leasing system is that the profit share is applied to positive profits only. In other words, the federal government does not bear any part of losses on non-commercial leases, whereas the profit share rate is in effect for successful leases. Exploration prospects will therefore look radically worse from the lessee's point of view than from the social point of view. The profit share system can therefore be expected to lead to a suboptimal level of exploration.

Administrative and Compliance Costs Under Profit Share Leasing. Companies differ in their level of efficiency. In order for the government to select the highest bidder, it should evaluate the probable efficiency of each competing bidder. But while this is desirable, it is also expensive and may be impossible in practice. This means that the company that bids the highest profit-share must be awarded the lease, even though that operator may not produce the most economic rent for the government.

In order to avoid the problems listed above, as well as others not listed, the government will probably attempt to police lessee operations extensively. This, of course, requires additional administrative costs. Furthermore, because the interpretation of profit is difficult, one must expect litigation of disputes entailing expensive attorney fees and court costs for both the operator and the government. All of these expenses further reduce available economic rents.

The General Accounting Office in a report to Congress has commented on the administrative costs of profit share leasing. Their analysis is summarized by the following passage from that report.

> While there is a wide variance in the oversight and additional recordkeeping and reporting responsibilities among the alternative systems, the fixed net

profit-share system is the only one projected to place extensive administrative burdens on Interior. For example, the fixed net profit-share system requires that audits be conducted on each producing tract. Interior officials estimate that accomplishing these audits may require from 0.5 to 3 staff years of effort. Assuming a $30,000 staff year, an audit could cost from $15,000 to $90,000. However, Interior officials have not yet identified who will be responsible for conducting the audits or the time interval. Some officials have stated that the audits should be conducted annually and that a longer interval may be adequate. Given these unknowns, and that a tract could have a producing life of 15 years or more, we estimate that the audit costs to Interior for one tract under this system, based on the 0.5 to 3 staff years estimate at $30,000 per staff year, could range between $225,000 and $1.35 million over the life of a lease.[13]

The GAO figures for audit costs are misleading and overstated because they failed to discount the annual audit costs incurred in future years. Nevertheless, if we accept GAO's annual cost estimates and the fifteen-year production life, at a reasonable discount rate the present value of audit costs over the life of each lease would still sum to between $184,000 and $1.11 million.[14] Other administrative costs would add still further to this total.

In their report to Congress, GAO also discussed the cost to the industry of compliance with a profit share leasing program. The GAO reported that it is the view of industry officials that profit share leasing would require the highest administrative costs of the alternative leasing systems. The GAO reported that "one company indicated that the accounting costs for this system could be as high as $200,000 per year over the life of the lease."[15]

The Interaction of Income Taxes and Profit Share Leasing.   The effect of income taxes upon a company operating a profit share lease may be considerable. Assuming that the marginal federal corporate tax rate is 46 percent,[16] the corporate tax coupled with a 30 percent profit-share bid results in an effective profit-share (or tax) rate of 62.2 percent. In this case, out of every additional dollar saved through efficiency, the company retains 37.8 cents. If an 80 percent profit-share bid is paired with a 46 percent corporate income tax, the effective tax rate is 89.2 percent. This leaves

13. Ibid., p. 51.
14. A 3 percent real discount rate was used in this computation.
15. See *note* 12 above, p. 51.
16. Forty-six percent is the current maximum federal marginal corporate tax rate.

only 10.8 cents for the firm out of each dollar saved as a reward for efficiency. This may be too small a ratio to produce reasonable efforts toward efficiency.

As in the case of royalty payments, profit share payments discourage investments in intensive reservoir management including well workovers, pressure maintenance projects, and secondary recovery investments, because losses on these investments are borne by the lessee alone. Some supermarginal investments will become submarginal and will be passed over. The lost net benefits are borne by the government in the form of reduced economic rents, and by all citizens in the form of resource waste.

Additional Problems of Profit Share Leasing. As with royalty leasing, firms submitting profit share bids are not required to disclose their actual production plans at the time of the auction. It is not economically valid to compare two profit-share bids when production is planned at different times. Finally, because there is no front-end payment, and the actual payment for a profit share lease occurs as production proceeds, profit share leasing may lead to unnecessary speculation at the expense of the federal government.

Empirical Evidence From Profit Share Lease Sales. Long-term experience with the profit share bidding system is limited to the state of California which, together with the city of Long Beach, has a record of oil production under profit share bidding arrangements beginning in 1965.[17] In the Long Beach case, the profit share bids for tracts in the sizable Wilmington field ranged from 95.56 percent for the major interest, to 100 percent for a minor working interest (see Table 4–2). The former was won by THUMS Long Beach Company.[18] This group was assigned operational responsibilities for the entire field. For this function, it receives a management fee amounting to 3 percent of all expenditures. While the high profit-share bids may appear to be a favorable arrangement for the lessor,[19] the profit share retained by the lease operators (after profit share payment, the 3 percent management fee, and income taxes) is only 0.75 percent. In effect, there is no efficiency incentive. As a substitute, the

17. More recently the state of Alaska has also issued leases using profit share leasing.

18. The THUMS Company is composed of Texaco, Humble (now Exxon), Union, Mobil, and Shell oil companies.

19. The Department of Oil Properties, City of Long Beach, Annual Report 35 (1965) proudly noted that "the City of Long Beach's record for obtaining unusually high revenue-producing contracts for developing the Tidelands is, according to available records, unequalled. . . . Because of this skill, citizens of Long Beach and the State of California receive maximum benefits."

Table 4–2. Winning Profit Share Bids, Long Beach Unit Working Interests, 1965.

Working Interest	No. of Bids	High Bid	Successful Bidder
(%)		(%)	
80.0	2	95.560	THUMS Long Beach Company
10.0	9	98.277	Pauley Petroleum and Allied Chemical
5.0	7	100.000	Standard Oil of California and Richfield Oil
2.5	8	99.540	Standard Oil of California and Richfield Oil
1.5	6	99.540	Standard Oil of California and Richfield Oil
1.0	6	99.550	Standard Oil of California and Richfield Oil
100.0	38	96.253	

SOURCE: City of Long Beach, Department of Oil Properties, Annual Report 1965, p. 35.

Department of Oil Properties has developed a fifty-person permanent staff to supervise and police the operators. Administrative interference with the operation of the field becomes a necessity. The Long Beach–Wilmington contract contains the following provision:

> The City Manager . . . shall exercise supervision and control of all day-to-day unit operations . . . and grant approvals in writing as he may deem appropriate for the supervision and direction of day-to-day operations of the Field Contractor, and the Field Contractor shall be bound by and shall perform in accordance with such determination. . . . [20]

One operator has stated that "hassle after hassle has developed regarding charges to the net profits account."[21]

The problem of poor cost control inherent in profit share bidding can be seen in the Long Beach leases. For example, the city of Long Beach has gone to great lengths to preserve the beauty of its coastline. Production in the Long Beach unit has occurred from three artificial islands in the tidelands. Each of these islands was constructed "under the close

20. Contractor's agreement, Article 14, Wilmington Oil Field, California, Long Beach unit.
21. Walter J. Mead, "Federal Public Lands Leasing Policies," *Colorado School of Mines Quarterly* 64 (Oct. 1969): 212.

supervision of the City Council and the City Manager, who have provided for design that both conceals oil operations and blends in with the natural beauty of the shoreline."[22] Considerable expenditures for landscaping, camouflaging and soundproofing oil derricks, sculptural forms, and other esthetic improvements were undertaken for each island.

In addition to beautifying the islands, the city has taken precautions to prevent environmental damage from tidelands oil operations. The city's policy in this area is summarized in this excerpt from one of its publications:

> The City of Long Beach, having a definite interest in the protection of its environment, has taken every precaution against oil leaks. From drilling to production and shipment, the City has insisted upon the most stringent controls. Our first consideration has always been the protection of our natural resources and, through our position as operator, we have been able to enforce these requests.[23]

To this end, the city has imposed a number of regulations on the offshore contractor, in some cases exceeding federal offshore standards. However, both the beautification and environmental protection expenditures undertaken on the Long Beach oil islands are 99.25 percent borne by the lessor because of the high profit-share rate. From a resource conservation perspective, the specified regulations and expenditures should not have been undertaken unless the value of the social benefits exceeded the social costs. There is no evidence that any such analysis was undertaken. Apparently, the city believed that the lessees were paying the cost and thus proceeded to mandate expenditures that would not have been approved under normal budgeting procedures.

The federal government has had limited recent experience with profit sharing as a component of the leasing system. In the federal leases issued after 1980, the bonus payment has been retained as the bid variable, but, the traditional one-sixth royalty payment has been replaced with a fixed net profit-share of not less than 30 percent. The fixed net profit-share has been used in nine lease sales.

As with larger royalty payments, part of the intent of profit share leasing is to encourage competition. An investigation by the GAO revealed that the use of a fixed net profit-share has actually reduced competition as measured by both the number of bidders and the number of companies participating in the auction. The reduction in participation was most pro-

---

22. Department of Oil Properties, City of Long Beach, "Long Beach's Oil Islands."
23. Ibid.

nounced among small companies. At the same time, the use of the fixed net profit-share also reduced the level of bonus bids relative to the traditional leasing method.[24] These preliminary findings would indicate that net profit-sharing has not been an effective method of offshore leasing.

In summary, while profit share bidding avoids some of the problems present in both bonus bidding and royalty bidding, it has its own set of serious drawbacks. Economic analysis indicates that economic rents received by the government will be substantially lower under profit share bidding than under bonus bidding.

WORK COMMITMENT LEASING

Under this system, the bidder specifies in detail the dollar amount he will commit for exploration in exchange for the lease, but the lessee is not required to spend the amount of the bid for exploration (see Chapter 1 for details). The disadvantages of this system are overwhelming.

The Disadvantages of Work Commitment Leasing

First, there is no practical way that the optimal exploration program on a lease can be known and specified in advance of drilling. An optimal program can be determined only after experience in drilling in a specific area is gained.

Second, the work commitment bidding system is an inefficient system during the exploration phase, as long as the dollar value of the work commitment has not been satisfied, because the lessee recovers one-half of his exploration costs from the federal government. Thus, the lessee's marginal cost of exploration is only half the social marginal cost. This implies that the lessee may continue his exploration efforts beyond the social optimum.

Third, if front-end loading has a negative impact on competition under bonus bidding, the problem is worse under the work commitment system than under the cash bonus system. To see this, consider the following example based on the present U.S. system. A lease offered for sale has an expected net present value of $10 million given an optimal exploration program of $5 million (in present value terms). The work commitment bid under conditions of effective competition would be $10 million plus one-half the cost of the exploration program, a total of $12.5 million. This amount is deposited with the federal government at the time of the lease

---

24. See *note* 12 above, p. 64.

auction, either in the form of a performance bond or in cash. Under cash bonus bidding with effective competition, the winning bid would be $10 million. The front-end payment required under the work commitment system is therefore greater than under cash bonus bidding.

Fourth, in the area of risk sharing, the U.S. work commitment system is also inferior to the cash bonus system, since the lessee forfeits to the federal treasury not only that part of the bid designed to cover economic rent, but also one-half of the value of the work program not undertaken. Thus, for a lease that turns out to be "hopeless" early in the exploration program and for which exploration is terminated earlier than anticipated, the payments made to the government will be higher than under the cash bonus system.

Finally, as with profit share leasing, any work commitment must be policed. Administrative costs of selecting the winning bidder and verifying the costs claimed will be very high. Correspondingly, the lessee must maintain added staff in order to negotiate with the government staff. These administrative costs are not part of the "necessary costs" of production but will be paid out of economic rent.

SUMMARY EVALUATION OF ALTERNATIVE LEASING SYSTEMS

In this chapter we have compared and analyzed three different leasing systems currently authorized for use in OCS lease sales. Table 4–3 summarizes our evaluation of the various bid variables with respect to the desirable attributes of a leasing system.

Royalty bidding has an advantage in terms of risk sharing and reduction of the front-end payment. It is less costly to administer than profit sharing because only revenues (or production) need be monitored. However, it has in common with profit sharing the shortcoming that the true high bidder cannot be identified in all cases. It has the further disadvantage of adversely affecting the production profile of the lease. Because royalty payments are treated as marginal production costs by the firms, production will be less than it would be in the absence of the royalty.

Profit share leasing has the advantage that if profit is properly defined, the production profile is unaffected by the leasing system. However, as a practical accounting problem, profit is hard to define precisely. Spillover benefits to the lessee firm or management may distort decision making. The government must carefully monitor both the revenues and the costs of the lessee firms to ensure compliance with the system. This problem

Table 4-3. Summary Evaluation of Alternative Bid Variables.

Bid Variable	Economic Efficiency	Fair Market Value	Selecting Most Efficient Firm	Risk Sharing	Administrative Costs
Cash bonus	Excellent. No postsale transfer payments.	Realized if competition is effective. High front-end payment.	Excellent if competition effective.	No risk sharing lessor/lessee. Risk exposure chosen by discretion of lessee.	Minimum
Royalty rate	Poor. Marginal prospects undeveloped, premature abandonment.	Effect of increase in competition unknown. No front-end payment.	Poor. Bids submitted in terms of rates.	Risk sharing lessor/lessee determined at auction.	Medium
Profit share	Fair. Suboptimal exploration, reduced incentive to control costs.	Effect of increase in competition unknown. No front-end payment.	Poor. Bids submitted in terms of rates.	Risk sharing lessor/lessee determined at auction. Lessor forces lessee into inferior joint venture contract.	High
Work commitment	Fair. Postsale subsidy of exploration. Development and production not affected by transfer payments.	Realized if competition effective. High front-end payment.	Excellent if competition effective.	Risk exposure chosen by discretion of lessee. Highest downside risk.	Medium

is further complicated by the fact that with high profit-shares, lessee firms have less incentive to control costs. With profit share leasing, administrative costs can be expected to be relatively high. Still another problem is that profit share bidding may award the lease to a firm other than the one that would produce the largest present value of economic rent. The reason for this is that profit share bids are submitted as rates, and the planned timing of production and the relative efficiency of the bidder are not disclosed. Finally, profit sharing as a means of risk sharing is inferior relative to joint bidding and joint venturing under the cash bonus system.

Work commitment leasing is an awkward system because it leads to the highest front-end payment, may cause excessive exploration, and imposes unnecessary administrative costs. Perhaps its single virtue is that, as specified in current federal regulations, and in common with bonus bidding, it tends to select the most efficient firm as the winning bidder.

5

ADDITIONAL ISSUES IN OFFSHORE LEASING

In chapters 3 and 4 we analyzed various methods of payment for offshore leases from the perspective of resource conservation. In this chapter we extend our analysis to other important offshore leasing issues.

First, we will consider the issue of expeditious development on the part of offshore lessees. In general, the government has tried to encourage speedy development of leases. We will consider the wisdom of this objective. Our analysis will include an investigation of rental payments and the primary lease term as they relate to expeditious development. We will also examine the impacts of the payment method and the postlease permit process on the diligence of OCS operators.

Next, we will turn our attention to the issue of the appropriate auction method for offshore leases. In particular, we will address the question of whether oral versus sealed bidding is preferred. This analysis will be followed by a discussion of the optimal tract size, in which we will ask if offshore leases are too small or too large.

Thereafter, we will examine the required minimum bid and bid rejection procedures of the Department of the Interior to determine whether they are necessary. Finally, we will discuss the nature of the political opposition to offshore leasing. In particular, we will look at opposition from state and local governments and from environmental groups. We will show under what circumstances such opposition is justified. We will explore alternatives in order to offer possible solutions to this conflict in leasing goals.

EXPEDITIOUS DEVELOPMENT OF OCS LEASES

Buyers of OCS oil and gas leases have long been encouraged, through the force of federal law and policy, to develop oil and gas resources "expeditiously." Both the language of the 1953 OCS Lands Act and the policy position of the Department of the Interior have been directed toward encouraging early drilling of leases and early field development of discoveries. Since the Arab oil embargo of 1973, the pressures for rapid development have been intensified in an effort to reduce crude oil imports. The 1978 OCS Lands Act Amendments spelled out explicitly the position of Congress: Expeditious development is a major goal of federal policy in regard to the OCS.

However, it is not clear what is meant by "expeditious" development. Generally, expeditious development has come to mean sooner rather than later development of a lease. More specifically, if oil or gas has been discovered in economic quantities, if pipelines and other production facilities are available, and if there are no legal or environmental barriers to production, the decision by a lessee to withhold production would be described by many as "nonexpeditious development." But this definition ignores a fundamental question, Is society made better off if leaseholders are pressed, through the force of law or policy, to increase the speed of development?

Economic theory does not necessarily favor sooner rather than later development where "sooner development" is defined in terms of speed in accomplishing early drilling, first production, or maximum production. Given free choice, a profit-maximizing OCS lessee will operate a lease with the objective of maximizing its present value. In some cases, profit maximization will be consistent with rapid development; in other cases, the attempt to develop leases more rapidly could lead to increased costs that might overwhelm the advantages of early receipt of revenues from production. If the present generation is consuming nonrenewable oil and gas resources too rapidly at the expense of future generations, then markets will signal future price increases for oil and gas, leading operators to delay present production. A delay in development in these two cases would represent a useful conservation of resources.

We define expeditious development as the production profile that is consistent with resource conservation. In the following sections, we will address two aspects of federal offshore lease contracts intended to speed development—rental payments and the primary lease term. Next, we will look at the unintended impact of the payment method for offshore leases on the timing of development. Finally we will examine the impact that federal regulations have on expeditious development.

Expeditious Development and Rental Payments

Lessees are required to make rental payments to the government on an annual basis beginning with the year in which a lease is issued and ending when production is large enough for the resulting royalty payments to exceed the amount of the fixed rental. Rental payments can be thought of as a penalty paid by the lessee for failure to drill upon, or exploit, a leased property. They are required, not for extracting the oil or gas, but for the privilege of deferring drilling and production operations for another year. For leases issued in the Gulf of Mexico, the annual rental payment has generally been set at $3 per acre per year. In some other areas of the OCS, rent is specified at $8 per hectare ($3.24 per acre) per year. While small in relation to bonus and royalty payments, rentals can be expected to become increasingly important if the government implements its planned acceleration in the leasing of offshore lands or if the primary lease term is generally lengthened.

Because rental payments can be avoided by beginning production, they tend to encourage early production from a lease. They do not, however, encourage resource conservation. Rental payments are viewed as costs by lessees, although they are actually transfer payments. As such they should not be allowed to alter production timing. From the perspective of resource conservation, the rental payments are unnecessary. To the extent that they alter timing decisions, they are undesirable.

Critics may argue that while OCS lands remain leased but unproductive, the government is entitled to some compensation. However, if the cash bonus is used as a bid variable at the auction, the inclusion of a rental payment has the effect of reducing the present value of the lease to prospective bidders, who, in turn, will reduce the level of their bids. For this reason, anticipated rental payments are not borne by the lessee, but are in fact borne by the lessor (in the form of lower bonus bids).

Expeditious Development and the Primary Lease Term

The primary lease term is the time period during which lessees are allowed to explore a lease tract. If oil is produced during this time, the lease term is routinely extended until production is finally terminated. The primary lease term for OCS oil and gas leases has generally been set at five years, although some recent leases in outlying frontier areas have had a ten-year term.

It is clearly the intent of the government to encourage early development of offshore leases through the imposition of a primary lease term. However, this encouragement is not without cost. Suppose that an unconstrained (with respect to production timing) firm chooses to develop a certain lease tract in twelve years and formulates its bonus bid on this basis. Next, suppose that the same firm is now constrained by a primary lease term of five years. In reformulating its bonus bid, the firm would adjust its bid downward to reflect the cost of the time constraint. Thus, the cost of encouraging early development is borne, at least in part, by the government itself.

This issue has increased in importance, given recent plans to step up the leasing of offshore lands. In fact, some individuals have advocated that all offshore mineral rights be placed in the hands of the private sector immediately. Such a policy, coupled with the relatively short five- to ten-year primary lease term, would reduce the total payment received by the government for the resource. If development of the resource is required in such a short period of time, bottlenecks would surely develop in acquiring the skilled labor and specialized capital equipment necessary for OCS exploration and production. Over a longer period of time, the markets for these inputs will adjust to increased demand, with more of the inputs being traded. However, in the short run, both labor and capital equipment are available in relatively inelastic supply. This means that the stimulus of more demand for the inputs would be felt primarily in higher input prices, with limited additional quantities of these inputs being provided to the market. The difference between the short-run and the long-run supply of inputs is illustrated in Figure 5-1. These higher input prices reduce the value of offshore leases. As a consequence, lessee firms will formulate lower bonus bids for these properties. In this case, a portion of the economic rent that could be collected by the federal government is diverted to the owners of specialized labor and capital inputs.

Privatization—An Alternative OCS Management Solution

One way to avoid this problem (and other problems in OCS management) is to eliminate the primary lease term altogether. The sale of mineral

Figure 5-1. Price of Exploration and Development Equipment With Accelerated Leasing.

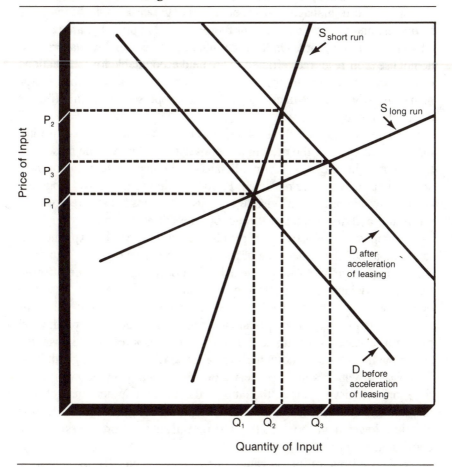

P₁, Q₁ represent the price and quantity of a factor of production traded before an acceleration in leasing offshore lands. P₂, Q₂ represent the price and quantity of a factor of production after an acceleration in leasing and retaining the 5-to-10-year primary lease term. P₃, Q₃ represent the situation if leasing is accelerated but the primary lease term is eliminated.

rights without a primary lease term is called *privatization* and amounts to shifting the management of resources from the public sector to the private sector.

There are many reasons to believe that private sector management may be preferable to public sector management. The first reason deals with the question of incentive—the difference between the incentive of private managers and that of public managers. With profit maximization as their motive, private managers have a strong incentive to use their resources efficiently. Those managers who obtain the greatest value from their resources, and who time the use of their resources optimally, are rewarded with maximum profit. On the other hand, private decision-makers who do not use their resources efficiently are held accountable for their actions by a direct reduction in their profits. Such is not the case for public sector managers, who are not likely to gain (or lose) personally from efficient decision-making.

Secondly, public sector decisions governing natural resource use are likely to unduly favor the present as opposed to the future. The reason for this "shortsightedness" is that politicians must consider the value of their actions in terms of being reelected. Politicians thus tend to favor programs (1) that provide near-term, visible benefits; (2) whose costs are borne in the future and are dispersed throughout the entire economy.

The imposition of a five-year primary lease term can be explained, at least in part, by the impatience of politicians to derive political gain from the leasing program. Once the decision has been made to issue offshore leases, politicians are eager to see immediate benefits. Private resource owners who are shortsighted in their resource management decisions reduce their profits. Under privatization, lessees choose the production profile of a lease to maximize the value of the resource. In this way the economic incentives of individuals are aligned with the public good. This is consistent with resource conservation. Additionally, by allowing more time for lease development, the labor and capital equipment markets can respond to increased demand for these inputs with increased production at prices lower than those that would prevail under more pressing time constraints.

Two criticisms of privatization are often voiced: (1) by removing undeveloped energy resources from the control of government, the needs of future generations will not be met; (2) the five-year lease term is necessary to avoid "speculative hoarding" of leases by large firms. Ironically the first of these criticisms implies that too much of the resource will be developed today, while the second implies exactly the opposite. Neither of these concerns is economically justified.

Suppose, for example, that the future reveals that (1) crude oil reserves are less than previously expected, (2) demand for crude oil is increasing at a faster rate than previously believed, or (3) backstop technologies such as shale oil, nuclear fission, or nuclear fusion (currently thought of as promising future energy sources) become unavailable. These events would indicate that future generations need more crude oil than previously expected; as a consequence, future crude oil prices would be expected to rise rapidly. Suppose that these new developments cause the value of crude oil *in situ* (in the ground) to rise at a 20 percent annual rate, and further, that the opportunity cost of capital is only 10 percent.[1] Under such conditions, profit-maximizing resource owners would find it in their interest to save more of their oil for future generations by producing less today. Such private decision-making would serve the general welfare in that resources would be more wisely allocated between present and future generations. Present prices of crude oil would, as a result, increase relative to future prices, leading users of crude oil and related products to seek out alternative energy sources (solar, wind, and the like) and to use less high-priced oil.

In spite of the fact that the market is able to respond properly to a perceived petroleum scarcity in the future, it may not be possible politically to eliminate the primary lease term. In our view, any lengthening of the lease term would be desirable. To the extent that the constraint cannot be significantly relaxed, the government collects less of its potential economic rent, and resources are allocated less efficiently between the present and future generations.

Expeditious Development and the Payment Method for OCS Leases

The traditional method of payment for OCS leases has been a cash bonus determined by public auction made at the time of the issuance of the lease, plus a 16⅔ percent royalty payment made from any subsequent production—or a rental payment in years when there is no production. More recently, a substantial number of offshore leases have been issued that place greater emphasis on the royalty as the method of lessee selection and payment. In particular, the royalty rate has been used as the bid variable in some OCS lease auctions, with resulting royalty rates as high as 82 percent. Leases have also been issued that retain the bonus payment as the bid variable but use a higher fixed royalty of 33⅓ percent, or a sliding scale royalty where the royalty rate varies between 16⅔ percent and 65 percent, depending on the level of production.

These higher royalty rates are inconsistent with the goal of expeditious development. As noted in Chapter 4, the higher royalty rates are viewed

---

1. The term *opportunity cost of capital* refers to the expected return on investment other than that due to holding oil reserves.

by the lessees as costs that can be partly avoided by delaying production. Thus, while the government has attempted to encourage early production through the imposition of rentals and primary lease terms of five to ten years, its move toward higher royalty rates is actually working counter to this objective. From the point of view of resource conservation and expeditious development, the optimal royalty rate is zero. Thus, it is our recommendation that rather than increase the royalty rate, the government should reduce it.

The Impact of Regulations on Expeditious Development

As noted in Chapter 1, the Santa Barbara oil spill in 1969 triggered substantial legislation designed to protect the environment from damage due to offshore oil and gas development. The effect of this legislation has been the creation of an extensive system of postlease approvals and permits that must be obtained before exploration, development, and production can commence, as well as government standards that must be met in the production process. Obtaining the required approvals and permits can be expensive and time-consuming. To the extent that this process is time-consuming, it is at variance with Congress's goal of expeditious development.

Federal Permits Issued by the USGS.   In obtaining the necessary approvals and permits, several federal agencies—as well as state and local agencies—may be involved. The federal agency with the single largest involvement is the U.S. Geological Survey, a division of the Department of the Interior. Prior to exploration of a lease tract, the lease operator must submit to the USGS a plan of exploration. The OCS Lands Act Amendments of 1978 require action by the USGS on a plan of exploration within approximately forty-two days of receipt of the plan. In addition to its own review, the USGS must consider, before approving the plan of exploration, comments submitted by the state adjacent to the lease tract. In a 1981 study of the permit process in the Gulf of Mexico region, the General Accounting Office noted that because "40 calendar days were required to process POE's [plans of exploration], *excluding State reviews,* GOMR [Gulf of Mexico Region] could be hard pressed to meet the 42 day maximum time frame established by OCSLAA [OCS Lands Act Amendments] regulations when State reviews are required."[2] In accordance with

2. U.S. General Accounting Office, Comptroller General's Report to Congress, *Impact of Regulations—After Federal Leasing—On Outer Continental Shelf Oil and Gas Development,* EMD-81-48, 27 Feb. 1981, p. 11, emphasis added.

the Coastal Zone Act of 1972, state coastal zone management agencies are allowed up to six months to review and comment on a plan of exploration. While the USGS can complete processing of the plan of exploration during this period, it cannot issue an operating permit until the state review is completed. Compliance with the Coastal Zone Management Act accords state governments a great deal of control over the federal OCS.

Following exploration, but prior to development, a second approval from the USGS is required for a plan of development. The OCS Lands Act Amendments grant the USGS 150 days to complete its review of a plan of development. This includes a period of sixty days for the adjacent state to comment on the plan. As with the review of a plan of exploration, the Coastal Zone Management Act also accords state agencies up to six months to review a plan of development.

Other Federal Permits.   In addition to the approval of the plans of exploration and development by the USGS, the lessee must also obtain permits from other federal agencies, including the Army Corps of Engineers, the Environmental Protection Agency, and the U.S. Coast Guard. The Army Corps of Engineers "issues permits that regulate: (1) installation of fixed structures (e.g., platforms, artificial islands) on the OCS; (2) discharges of dredged material into U.S. waters; and (3) transportation of dredged materials for purposes of ocean dumping."[3] The time required for the corps to grant its permit is not limited by federal law and can extend to well over a year.

The Environmental Protection Agency administers the National Pollutant Discharge Elimination System (NPDES) in accordance with section 402 of the Clean Water Act as amended in 1977. In this capacity, it issues permits to OCS lessees that allow drilling mud and cuttings, and other nontoxic effluents, to be discharged offshore. The potential delays and additional costs in lease development due to the NPDES process are chronicled in the following story from a GAO report.

> Mobil Oil was drilling on tracts that it had acquired in December 1975—OCS lease Sale 35. After acquiring additional OCS tracts in a June 1979 lease sale—OCS lease Sale 48—Mobil submitted an application to EPA on August 14, 1979, to extend its drilling authority to include adjacent OCS Sale 48 tracts. On October 18, 1979, EPA issued notice that an NPDES permit would be given to Mobil in 30 days. Before the permits were issued, however, several interested parties asked for a public hearing. The hearing was held on January 17, 1980. No one testifying against issuance of the permit offered any evidence

---

3. Ibid., p. 16.

that environmental harm would result from exploratory drilling in the Sale 48 area and the hearing officer stated that a permit would be issued.

After another EPA administrative delay, the NPDES permit was issued on February 14, 1980, but was not effective for another 30 days to provide another comment period. In mid-March a group called Scenic Shoreline Preservation requested an evidentiary hearing challenging the permit. EPA's procedural regulations require a party objecting to an NPDES permit to present evidence which indicates why a permit should not be issued. If this burden is not met, the interested party is not entitled to an evidentiary hearing. EPA's regional personnel agreed with the request, even though no new evidence indicating environmental harm was presented to lend support to this decision.

According to Mobil, from the date it first applied to EPA for a NPDES permit modification until EPA decided to hold an evidentiary hearing, took about 7 months and cost Mobil about $2 million. An evidentiary hearing has still not been scheduled. Mobil has started exploratory drilling in the Sale 48 area and is barging the drilling muds and cuttings to an onshore dumping site, which is more costly and, Mobil also believes, more environmentally hazardous.[4]

The U.S. Coast Guard issues navigational aid permits, and inspects and certifies all mobile drilling units and vessels. While these permits are generally issued in a few days, some can take much longer. One such permit required 211 days to be issued.[5]

State and Local Permits.   In addition to permits issued by federal agencies, state and local agencies are also involved in the permit process. State and local agencies may grant permits for access and right of way through state waters, and for shoreline facilities designed for storage and processing. As noted earlier, states are also allowed input in the approval of plans of exploration and plans of development. Additionally they may contribute to NPDES and Army Corps of Engineer permits.

Expeditious Development and the Permit Process.   Clearly the large number of required postlease permits may seriously delay the development of a lease. The delays are likely to become longer as more controversial and environmentally sensitive areas are leased. The economic rationale for the permit process is to correct for possible external costs that may result from oil and gas development. However, the process appears to create new and costly externalities. The benefits from OCS

4. Ibid., pp. 33–34.
5. Ibid., p. 18.

operations accrue to the nation as a whole. The adjacent state receives only its proportionate share. But the costs of any oil spill and the costs of school, police, highways, and other support services are borne primarily by state and local governments. Thus, adjacent communities may have an incentive to delay or avoid entirely any exploration and production activities off their shores, even if those activities are beneficial to the nation as a whole. The permit process accords these local jurisdictions the opportunity to impose delays.

The permit process requires bureaucratic costs for issuing the permits and monitoring compliance with their provisions; also entailed are costs to the lessees from the delay of production and the preparation of permit applications. The bureaucratic costs are borne directly by the government. Furthermore, the present value of the compliance costs known to the lessees at the date of the auction are deducted from bid values. Thus, the government will generally pay the full cost of delays, permits, and regulations. Economic theory suggests that each type of permit and regulation be submitted to the rigors of benefit-cost analysis to determine whether society benefits from the process. Permits and regulations that do not pass this test should be eliminated.

THE AUCTION METHOD—ORAL VERSUS SEALED BIDDING

While the required auction method at federal OCS sales is sealed bidding, current regulations frequently allow the use of either oral or sealed bidding in issuing mineral leases for onshore properties, and various state governments employ oral bidding to issue oil and gas leases.[6] In addition, the U.S. Forest Service and the Bureau of Land Management rely on oral bidding to sell timber from the national forests and other public lands.

Economic theory predicts that sealed bidding is more effective in collecting economic rent when there is uncertainty regarding the level of competition. There are several reasons for this. First, in an oral auction, the winning bid is slightly greater than the bid of the second highest bidder. All prospective bidders must be in attendance at the auction. Bidding normally begins at a prestated minimum level, with prospective buyers allowed to rebid if they desire. The bidding ends when no higher bid is made. Thus the winning bidders in an oral auction need not necessarily

6. Walter J. Mead, "Natural Resource Disposal Policy—Oral Versus Sealed Bidding," *Natural Resources Journal* 7 (April 1967): 198.

bid their true valuation of the tract; they need only outbid the next highest bidder.

With sealed bidding, prospective buyers are more likely to bid their true valuation of the lease. In this format, firms are allowed to submit only one bid, and all bids are to be opened at a prespecified date. The lease is awarded to the highest bidder, who need not be present. While at oral auctions each bidder knows the identity and bid level of his competitors, this is not the case at sealed bid auctions. In preparing a bid for a sealed bid auction, the bidder cannot be sure how many competitors there will be and what they will bid. Even when only one bid is submitted, this bid is more likely to reflect the full valuation of the lease. At sealed bid auctions, there is often a large amount of "money left on the table." Money left on the table is defined as the difference between the highest and second highest bid. Viewed with hindsight, it is money spent unnecessarily to acquire a lease. The record amount of money left on the table was $172.4 million when Chevron and Phillips bid $333.6 million for a Santa Maria Basin lease offshore California in 1981. The second high bid, $161.2 million, was submitted by Standard Oil of Indiana.

Second, while collusive arrangements among prospective bidders are possible under either oral or sealed bidding, with oral auctions it is easier for conspirators to signal one another and thus police their collusive arrangements. If an effective collusion exists among bidders, the bidding is constrained and the high bid does not necessarily reflect the true value of the asset. To the extent that collusion among buyers is easier under oral bidding, the level of bids is lower.

The advantages of sealed bidding over oral bidding are greatest if the level of competition is weak. If there is vigorous competition, it is likely that the bid of the second high bidder will be closer to the valuation of the high bidder. Thus, the "money left on the table" will generally be smaller in areas of greater competition. Additionally, the greater the number of competitors, the more difficult it is to maintain collusive arrangements. On both these counts, the advantages of sealed bidding are likely to be fewer if competition is strong.

A real-world test of the economic predictions concerning oral versus sealed bidding was made possible by changes in the legislation governing U.S. Forest Service timber sales during the 1970s. Prior to 1976, the vast majority of the timber sales conducted in the Pacific Northwest utilized oral bidding. In October 1976, the National Forest Management Act mandated the expanded use of sealed bidding in timber sales. In the spring of 1978, this legislation was amended and historical bidding procedures were restored. During the period from October 1976 through March 1978, 53.2 percent of the 1,270 timber sales in the Douglas fir and Ponderosa pine subregions of the Pacific Northwest (Region 6) were conducted using sealed bidding.[7]

In a statistical study of these sales, Mead, Schniepp, and Watson found that after correcting for other variables affecting the level of winning bids, the use of sealed bidding increased the level of winning bids in eight of the nine forests in the Douglas fir subregion and in eight of the eleven forests in the Ponderosa pine subregion.[8,9] Overall, the use of sealed bidding increased the winning bids in these regions by an average of $13.68 and $3.34 per thousand board feet, respectively.[10] These results led the authors to conclude that "competition has been strengthened by sealed bidding methods."[11]

One drawback of sealed bidding relative to oral bidding stems from the fact that a firm with capital constraints can submit sealed bids for only a limited number of leases. Although the firm may win none of the leases for which it has bid, it cannot bid on more tracts because of the risk of buying more leases than it can pay for. At oral auctions, on the other hand, if a bidder is unsuccessful in competing for one lease, he is still able to bid for subsequent leases. In this way, oral bidding may facilitate competition for lease tracts.

Stephen McDonald, recognizing this drawback in sealed bidding, has suggested an adjustment to existing sealed bidding procedures.

The remedy is to permit what may be called sequential bidding. After a tentative closing of bidding in a sale, bids would be opened for individual tracts in the order of the number of bids per tract. Drawings would be held in the case of ties. The winning bid for each tract would be announced, but not the identity of the winner; the losers (or winner) would be permitted to submit new bids on other tracts in the sale before bids on the latter were opened. This system would increase the cumbersomeness of a large lease sale, but it would

7. Walter J. Mead, Mark Schniepp, and Richard B. Watson, *The Effectiveness of Competition and Appraisals in the Auction Markets for National Forest Timber in the Pacific Northwest,* USFS Contract No. 53-3187-1-43 and PSW G-34, 30 Sept. 1981, pp. 218, 227.

8. Ibid., p. 226. Four of the national forests show significant positive impacts at the .10 level, two of which are significant at the .01 level.

9. Ibid., p. 231. Two of the national forests show significant positive impacts at the .10 level, one of which is significant at the .01 level; two of the forests indicate significant negative impacts at the .01 level.

10. Ibid., pp. 226, 231. The coefficient for sealed bidding was significant at the .01 level for the Douglas fir region.

11. Ibid., p. viii.

increase the average number of bids per tract and tend to result in higher winning bids under uncertainty, to say nothing of increasing the scope of opportunity for relatively small firms. The effective increase in competition would make it more likely that the government captures all the pure economic rent.[12]

THE OPTIMAL TRACT SIZE

The size of the OCS leases is currently limited to a maximum of 5,760 acres (9 square miles).[13] There is some disagreement as to whether this size is too large or too small.

On the one hand, there are those who believe that leases of 5,760 acres are too large. Their argument is generally based on the impact that lease size has on the level of bonus bids. Assuming that the tract size and lease value are positively correlated, the larger the lease size, the larger the lease value, and thus the larger the bonus bid. But as noted in Chapter 3, larger bonus bids are suspected by some as posing a barrier to participation of smaller firms. If so, large tract sizes reduce competition, thus reducing the return to government. Our earlier empirical analysis of bonus bidding has shown that at current lease sizes, the level of bonus bids has not prevented the government from receiving fair value for its leases.

On the other hand, there are those who believe that current lease sizes are too small. The principal reason for this belief is that some development and production externalities are not internalized when lease sizes are too small. These externalities are the result of the migratory nature of oil and gas. Once oil and gas are discovered on a single reservoir, each lessee has an economic incentive to develop and produce from each tract as quickly as possible (too fast for efficient operation).

There are two methods of dealing with this problem, both of which require that the externalities be internalized. One method is to increase tract size.[14] A second method is through postlease unitization of leases that overlie a field, or through the acquisition of the production rights to adja-

12. Stephen L. McDonald, "Federal Energy Resource Leasing Policy," in Walter J. Mead and Albert E. Utton, eds., *U.S. Energy Policy: Errors of the Past, Proposals for the Future* (Cambridge, Mass.: Ballinger Publishing Co., 1979), p. 48.

13. 43 U.S.C. 1337(b).

14. See Frederick M. Peterson, "The Government Role in Mineral Exploration," in Michael Crommelin and Andrew R. Thompson, eds., *Mineral Leasing as an Instrument of Public Policy* (Vancouver: University of British Columbia Press for The British Institute for Economic Policy Analysis, 1977), pp. 150–51; and Frederick M. Peterson, "Two Externalities in Petroleum Exploration," in Gerard M. Brannon, ed., *Studies in Energy Tax Policy* (Cambridge, Mass.: Ballinger Publishing Co., 1975), pp. 101–2.

cent leases by one lessee through the postlease assignment market. We have found that 206 tracts were included in the thirty-five development units in existence as of March 1978. Thus each development unit was composed of an average of 5.9 leases. Would the lessees have paid more for these tracts if the initial lease sizes were larger and they could have avoided the costs of unitization? To our knowledge no research relating to this question has been conducted. Such research is needed if the government is to select a tract-size policy that maximizes economic rent collection.

THE MINIMUM BID AND BID REJECTION PROCEDURES

As previously noted, OCS lease auctions have traditionally used a sealed bonus bid as the bid variable. However, the highest bidder at the time the bids are opened is not necessarily granted the option to explore and develop the lease tract because the Interior Department has the statutory authority to reject any or all bids. First, the bids must exceed the established minimum bid requirements. For wildcat leases the minimum bid has recently been increased sixfold, from $25 to $150 per acre.[15] While $150 per acre does not seem like a large sum of money, when multiplied by a lease size in the thousands of acres, it can amount to a considerable sum for a property near which no viable oil and gas prospects have been previously located. Recall that the maximum lease size is 5,760 acres, with many leases at or approaching that size. For a lease of the maximum size, the minimum bid is $864,000! As we have previously shown, 61.57 percent of the Gulf of Mexico leases issued from 1954 through 1969 recorded no production and were returned to the government. Under these circumstances, it is not surprising that many of the tracts offered in frontier areas attract no bids.

It should be further noted that the minimum bid rate is invariant to the type and size of the bid variable used at the lease auction. While the traditional bonus bid system carries a royalty requirement of one-sixth of the gross value of future production, many of the alternative leasing systems mandated by the OCS Lands Act Amendments of 1978 require larger royalty rates. At the time of the auction, profit-maximizing prospective lessees deduct the expected present value of future royalty payments— along with other exploration, development, regulatory, and production costs—from expected gross revenues to arrive at the level of their bids.

---

15. Department of the Interior, Mineral Management Service, "Interior Department Announces New OCS Bid Adequacy Procedures," news release, 10 March 1983.

If royalty rates are increased, other factors being held constant, the level of bonus bids is reduced, thus making it more difficult for firms to meet the minimum bid requirement.

The stated objective of the minimum bid requirement is to "assure the public of fair value for the development of the resources."[16] But as a practical matter, the policy is designed to insulate the federal government from accusations of "giving away" the mineral rights to offshore areas. Rather than looking at returns from the federal leasing program in the aggregate, the government is embarrassed when an occasional wildcat lease turns out to be of substantially greater value than its bonus, rental, and royalty payments. It is quickly forgotten that frontier areas are frequently of relatively little or no value.

Suppose, for example, that in evaluating a 5,000 acre tract, five prospective lessees arrive at the conclusion that it is worth approximately $500,000, give or take $50,000 depending on the lessee (representing the risk-adjusted, expected value of the lease). A lease tract of this size would have a minimum bid of $750,000. Under these circumstances, the lessees would submit no bids for the tract. But this does not serve the public interest. The public is denied the bonus bid and the potential oil and gas that might be discovered on the tract. Regrettably, it is worthwhile for bureaucratic administrators to forgo the bonus payment (for which they receive no personal reward) to ensure that they will not be accused by an angry public of not collecting fair market value for offshore leases.

Even if the bidding exceeds the required minimum level, there is no guarantee that the lease will actually be issued: The Interior Department may still reject the bids as inadequate. The department has recently revised its bid adequacy procedures. The process has been decentralized so that the determination of whether bids are adequate is made in the regional offices of the Minerals Management Service (MMS), an agency of the Department of the Interior, rather than in Washington.[17]

The decision to accept or reject bids is based on a variety of information including the high bid, the "mean range of values" (MROV), the "discounted mean range of values" (DMROV), and the "geometric average evaluation of tract" (GAEOT).[18] While the high bid is self-explanatory, the other variables listed above require more explanation.

The MROV is the MMS estimate of the fair bonus value of a tract. The

16. Ibid.

17. Ibid.

18. Department of the Interior, Mineral Management Service, "Post-Sale Analysis Summary for OCS Sale 69 (Part II)," Sale Specific Data Series 3/Number 4, 14 March 1983.

MMS collects geological, engineering, and economic data about a lease and uses a statistical technique known as Monte Carlo simulation to generate a set of fair bonus values for the tract. The MROV is the mean or average of the bonus values of the Monte Carlo simulation. If the MROV as calculated above is less than $150 per acre, MMS equates the MROV to the minimum bid ($150 per acre, see above).[19]

The DMROV is closely related to the MROV. At the time that the MROV is calculated, MMS also calculates the mean of the range of values of the lease *if it were leased one year later.* This number is then discounted to the present time period, yielding the DMROV. The idea behind this variable is to determine whether it is in the government's interest to wait another year before issuing the lease.[20]

Finally, the MMS calculates the GAEOT. The GAEOT is the geometric mean of the bids received on the tract and the MROV. It is expressed algebraically as follows:

$$GAEOT = (B1 \cdot B2 \cdot B3 \cdot \ldots \cdot Bn \cdot MROV) \cdot exp(1/(n+1))$$

where Bi is the ith bid and n is the total number of bidders. The GAEOT summarizes (or is a measure of central tendency) of evaluations of the tract given by all the bidders and the MMS.[21]

As with the minimum bid requirement, the bid adequacy procedures are intended to ensure that the federal government receives fair market value for OCS oil and gas development rights. But in the presence of effective competition, such procedures are unnecessary. The market will guarantee that the government will receive fair market value for its leases. Even if lessees were initially able to make excessive profits on their offshore leases, this would quickly attract new participants into the OCS lease market, with the result that, in the long run, only a normal rate of return would be earned. Our empirical analysis of the 1,223 Gulf of Mexico OCS leases issued from 1954 through 1969 indicates that OCS lessees have not been able to earn excessive profits over the long run (see Chapter 3).

There are many commentators who believe competition is ineffective when there are few bidders. They point to a number of recent lease sales in which only one bid was received. But, the number of bidders is not only an indicator of the level of competition; it is also a proxy for the

19. Ibid.
20. Ibid.
21. Ibid.

perceived quality of the lease. Leases of expected low quality will quite naturally attract few bidders. Additionally, the number of bids received at a sealed bid auction is only a proxy for the perceived competition for the lease. If prospective lessees believe that there is substantial competition for a lease tract, even if only one bid is received at the auction, the auction may still yield competitive results and return the available economic rent to the government.

STATE OBJECTIONS TO FEDERAL OFFSHORE LEASING

The production of oil and gas from the OCS can be thought of as a federal project with huge net national benefits. While it is doubtful that production of OCS oil will alter the price of crude oil, since this price is determined by worldwide market forces, the nation benefits from offshore production to the extent that it can substitute domestic production at a lower cost than the price of imported crude oil.[22] These benefits are illustrated in Figure 5-2.

At the world market price of crude oil, approximately $30 per barrel in August 1984, imported oil is available in what is effectively perfectly elastic supply.[23] This means that domestic consumers of imported oil perceive that they can import as much oil as desired at the world price. Total domestic crude oil consumption is given by the intersection of the perfectly elastic supply curve of imported oil, S_i, with the domestic demand curve, D, at Q^*. The portion of Q^* that would be produced domestically in the absence of OCS production is Q^1. With OCS production, the domestic supply curve shifts outward, resulting in Q^2 being produced domestically. The difference between these two domestic production levels, $Q^2 - Q^1$, is the reduction in imports that results from opening the OCS for exploration and development.

Although the national net benefits from OCS production are obviously large, there is tremendous state and local resistance to offshore leasing. The opposition to offshore leasing is particularly strong in California and Alaska. The reason for these conflicts is found in the distribution of net benefits. For most federal projects, the benefits accrue primarily within a small area of the country, while the costs are widely dispersed across the entire nation. OCS leasing is of exactly the opposite nature—the

---

22. *Cost* here is defined as social opportunity cost, which includes environmental and user cost.

23. The market supply curve for crude oil is not perfectly elastic, but it is the perception of importers of crude oil that as individuals their actions have little effect on the market price. For expositional ease, we shall assume there is a perfectly elastic supply of imported oil.

Figure 5-2. Domestic Production With and Without OCS Production.

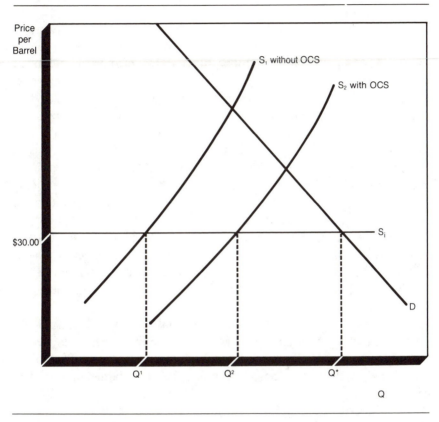

benefits are highly dispersed and the costs are localized. In this situation, the political process does not allocate resources efficiently.

The political system allocates too many resources to the traditional type of project. Consider a federal water project whose cost, when viewed from a national perspective, is not justified by its benefits. The project may still be funded by Congress because the special interests who benefit from such a project are well organized politically and are able to pledge support, in the form of campaign funds and votes, to politicians who favor the project. The political interests of those who must bear the project's costs, the nation as a whole, are not represented in an organized way. Assuming that such a water project would cost each citizen of the United States a nominal sum (e.g., 25 cents), it would not be rational for groups of citizens to organize politically or for individual citizens to become informed on such issues.[24] As a consequence, politicians nationwide may support such projects with impunity, even if they are aware that the projects are not in the national interest.

In the area of offshore leasing, the groups that are well organized politically consist of local citizens who must bear a disproportionate share of the costs. In particular, the groups allied against offshore development are state and local governments and environmentalists. State and local governments oppose offshore leasing because much of the cost of services that support these activities must be borne by local residents. Such services include police and fire protection, maintenance of streets and highways, additional schools, and the like. There is some local benefit from increased economic activity in the region in the form of more jobs, higher incomes, and possibly increases in the tax base, but these benefits may not offset the increased costs. The benefits from OCS oil production are shared with the nation as a whole. In a 1981 study of the regional impacts of federal offshore leasing on the state of Alaska, Porter and Huskey estimated that the total net burden on the original residents of Alaska (those people who were in residence prior to the federal offshore leasing) lies between $917 and $2,309 per capita.[25] It is not surprising, then, that local citizens would oppose offshore leasing.

One method of circumventing state objections to offshore leasing would be for the federal government to share part of the revenue from the leases with each adjacent state. In order to gain state support, the payments would have to be large enough to offset the costs borne by the local residents. Such payments do not affect resource conservation. Rather, they redistribute the benefits of offshore leasing.

At the present time, the federal government is considering a program of OCS revenue sharing with adjacent states. Such a program already exists for revenues derived from federal timber sales. For OCS leasing, the program might include the sharing of bonus revenue or of bonus plus royalty revenue. Of these options, the most effective would be a sharing of all offshore leasing revenue. If bonus payments alone were shared, states might support the leasing of the OCS but, since they would have no stake in subsequent development, might wish to delay exploration and development.

24. This phenomenon has been referred to as "rational ignorance." See J. Gwartney and R. Stroup, *Economics: Private and Public Choice* (Orlando, Fla.: Academic Press, 1983).

25. Ed Porter and Lee Huskey, "The Regional Economic Effect of Federal OCS Leasing: The Case of Alaska," *Land Economics* 57 (no. 4, Nov. 1981): 594.

ENVIRONMENTALIST OBJECTIONS TO FEDERAL OFFSHORE LEASING

The estimates of the net burden to local citizens of offshore leasing cited above do not include the possible adverse environmental effects of offshore leasing. Environmental groups have been highly critical of offshore leasing policy. To the extent that offshore oil and gas exploration and development generate external costs not internalized by the lessees, environmentalist concerns may be warranted. The problem is illustrated in Figure 5–3.

Figure 5–3. The Effects of External Costs on Offshore Production.

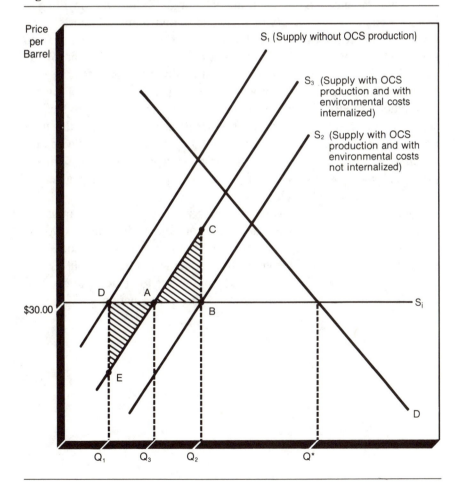

As noted above, the domestic production including OCS oil and gas is given as Q_2, derived from the domestic supply curve S_2. But suppose that S_2 does not take into account the full costs of production because external environmental costs are not included. In this situation, at Q_2 the total marginal costs of production exceed the price at which oil can be imported; thus resources are not conserved. The total cost to society resulting from excessive OCS development is the area of the triangle ABC. Resource conservation is attained at output level Q_3, derived by using the supply curve S_3, which includes external costs. At Q_3 there may be some environmental damage, but the benefits of the oil and gas produced are sufficient to outweigh the costs. Environmentalists would be justified in seeking reductions in output from Q_2 to Q_3. Unfortunately, many environmentalists and environmental organizations are unwilling to balance economic costs (which include environmental costs) and economic benefits; they would allow only offshore activities that pose "no significant damage" to the environment *regardless of the benefit*. When carried to the extreme, this policy would totally eliminate offshore production (and much onshore production as well). The results of such a prohibition are also shown in Figure 5–3. With no offshore production, supply would shift to S_1 and production would shrink to Q_1. But this does not conserve resources because additional output (up to Q_3) could be produced at a lower cost, including environmental costs, than the import price. The total loss to society of producing too little output is given by the area of the triangle *ADE*.

Some would argue that when managing resources as important as the OCS, it is best to err on the side of environmentalism. This position is inconsistent with resource conservation. It is just as costly to society to waste a dollar's worth of resources by producing too little output as it is to waste a dollar's worth of resources by producing too much output. Both types of errors reduce the standard of living of the nation.

6

SUMMARY, CONCLUSIONS, AND RECOMMENDATIONS

We share the view of most Americans that conservation should be the main concern of natural resource management. The economic definition of resource conservation requires that the present value of the economic rent of a resource be maximized. Furthermore, as the owners of the resource, the American people should collect this value as payment for the right to develop mineral resources on public lands. However, it is important to realize that the policies adopted by government agencies in managing natural resources affect the value of their economic rent through the way in which they affect economic incentives. Thus, in formulating natural resource management policies, the incentives created by each policy should be considered. In the preceding chapters we have analyzed a number of the federal government's OCS management policies from the perspective of resource conservation and have tried to uncover the intended and unintended effects that these policies have had on the incentives facing lessees. Current policies and our recommendations are summarized in Table 6-1 and are discussed below.

Applying the economic meaning of conservation to the various government-authorized methods of payment for offshore leases has led us to the conclusion that while no payment method is perfect, the cash bonus is the preferred method of both payment and lessee selection. The primary advantages of such a system stem from the way lessee firms look at bonus payments. Because these payments are made at the time a lease

Table 6–1. Summary of Existing OCS Lease Policies and Recommendations.

Leasing Issue	Current Policy	Recommended Policy
a. Method of payment	Cash bonus with one-sixth fixed royalty	Cash bonus
b. Auction method	Sealed bidding	Sealed sequential bidding
c. Expeditious development	Rental payment (usually $3 per acre)	Eliminate rental payment
	Primary lease term (usually 5 years)	Eliminate primary lease term
d. Lease size	Maximum 5,670 acres with postlease unitization	Allow larger lease size to include expected reservoir
e. Revenue sharing with adjacent state	Minimal	Expand revenue sharing to cover costs borne by adjacent state
f. Environmental concerns	Various federal, state, and local regulations and permits	Retain regulations and permits whose benefits exceed their costs

is issued, they are viewed by lessees—when subsequent exploration and development decisions are made—as a sunk cost. As such they do not affect the marginal decision-making of the firm. Assuming that all costs and benefits are internalized, the incentives of the lessee are aligned with the public interest. The principal criticism of the cash bonus as a lease payment method has not been based on its resource conservation properties, but rather on the belief that it may not return fair value to the government for offshore leases. This income distribution issue can be investigated empirically. We have found that in fact the level of competition for OCS leases has been sufficient to prevent lessees, in the aggregate, from making more than a normal rate of return on their offshore investments.

Given these theoretical and empirical findings, it would appear that the provisions of the OCS Lands Act Amendments of 1978 (OCSLAA) mandating the use of alternative leasing systems on a trial basis were based on the faulty premise that the existing leasing system was not working well. Nevertheless, the OCSLAA did authorize the use of royalty, profit share, and work commitment leasing. Of these, profit share leasing has received the support of some economists. Profit share payments are only slightly inferior to bonus payments in their effects on marginal decision-making, depending on how profit is defined in the lease contract. Furthermore, profit share leasing does not require from lessees a large "front-end" payment, which may encourage competition; and profit share payments are more closely correlated with actual tract values than are bonus payments on a tract-specific basis. However, profit share leasing also has two large disadvantages relative to bonus bid leasing. First, profit is difficult to define. Under such a system, lessees have an incentive to overstate costs and understate revenues, while the opposite is true for lessors. This means that disputes are likely to arise between lessees and lessors regarding the actual level of profit. The results of these conflicts are large monitoring and policing costs on the part of the government and large compliance costs on the part of the lessees. A second problem of profit share leasing is that by itself it cannot unambiguously select the most efficient firm to operate a lease. This is not a problem with bonus bid leasing.

Royalty leasing has advantages and disadvantages similar to profit share leasing. The problem of administrative and compliance costs under royalty leasing are not as severe as those under profit share leasing in that only production needs to be monitored. However, the most serious defect of royalty leasing is that, unlike bonus and profit share payments, royalty payments affect marginal decision-making and, as a consequence, alter production and timing decisions. In particular, royalty payments induce the slowing of production and lead to the premature abandonment of a lease.

Work commitment leasing is the least desirable of the alternatives authorized by the OCSLAA. Its disadvantages were apparently obvious to the Department of the Interior, and it was not used during the trial period ending in 1983. Given the theoretical advantages of bonus bidding and the empirical finding that it has returned fair value to the government for OCS leases in the aggregate, we believe that it is the best payment method.

Turning to the auction method, the federal government is required by statute to issue OCS leases using sealed bidding. We believe this is wise. The alternative, oral bidding, is effective when the number of bidders is large, but is not as effective as sealed bidding when there are few bidders (as may be the case for wildcat OCS leases). This result is supported empirically by the experience of the U.S. Forest Service in selling public timber in the Pacific Northwest, namely, that sealed bidding increased the winning bids.

One disadvantage of sealed bidding, as it is now conducted for OCS leases, stems from the manner in which the bids are collected and tabulated. At each lease sale a number of tracts are offered for bid. The sealed bids for all tracts must be submitted by a prespecified date, and all bids for all tracts are subsequently opened and recorded at the same time. If a bidder is unsuccessful in his attempt to acquire one lease, he is not able, at that point, to submit new bids on other leases offered in the same sale because of the institutional framework of the sale procedure. A recommended solution to this problem, sequential bidding, is for the tracts at a particular sale to be sold in order of the number of bids received. This gives losing bidders the opportunity to submit bids for subsequent leases offered at the same sale and may increase the number of bids.

One concern that the government has frequently voiced is that leases, once issued, be developed expeditiously. To this end, two policies have been developed: the rental payment and the primary lease term. While both policies have the effect of accelerating OCS development, there remains a fundamental question of whether any policy that encourages early development is in the public interest. Economic theory suggests that the market will accelerate exploration and production through adjustments in the price of a resource if (in present value terms) current generations value a resource more highly than do the future generations. In order to take advantage of these economic forces, it is not desirable or necessary to impose diligence requirements. One way to use these forces is to eliminate rental payments and the primary lease term. Such a policy has received some attention recently and is referred to as privatization. There are many resource conservation reasons for believing that private sector ownership of offshore mineral rights is preferable to public sector ownership. From an economic perspective, the case for privatization is strong. The principal impediment to its adoption is political. Political support is lacking primarily because there is no public awareness of its resource conservation benefits.

The current maximum size of offshore leases is 5,670 acres. This size is sometimes not large enough to internalize all the costs and benefits of oil and gas exploration and production. One way of eliminating this problem is to require the unitization of tracts that encompass a reservoir. A second method is to expand the initial tract size to include the expected reservoir. Of the two, the latter method has the advantage of avoiding the transaction costs of unitization.

The primary political opposition to offshore leasing comes from adjacent state and local governments and from environmental organizations. State and local governments are not at present entitled to any of the revenues received from federal leases. Nevertheless, a portion of the cost of offshore development is borne by these agencies in providing the public goods that support these activities. One suggested solution to this conflict is for the federal government to share OCS lease revenues with the adjacent states. While the redistribution of the revenues from offshore leasing does not directly affect the economic rent from the resource, such a program of revenue sharing would reduce state opposition to federal leasing—provided that the revenues received by the states are large enough to offset the costs they incur in providing services for offshore development and for accepting the risk of oil spills and environmental pollution.

The concerns of environmentalists are derived from the observation that some of the environmental costs of OCS development are not borne by the lessee firms. If negative externalities are present, private developers will tend to produce more OCS resources than are socially desirable. The correction of market failures due to externalities is one of the primary justifications of government. However, there are some environmentalists who take the view that no environmental damage is acceptable *regardless of the benefits of offshore leasing.* This view is not consistent with resource conservation. Policies designed to protect the environment only serve the public if the benefits they create are in excess of their costs. Typically, such an evaluation of the costs and benefits of environmental regulations is not conducted. Resource conservation requires that all environmental regulations be submitted to the rigors of benefit-cost analysis, and only those which result in a net benefit to society be retained.

One of the most important fruits of the labors of economic theorists of the last two hundred years has been the discovery that under conditions of competition and insignificant externalities, the economic incentives governing the actions of private individuals are consistent with resource conservation. However, although it may be demonstrated that the market for a particular resource is effectively competitive, public managers historically have not trusted the private sector to manage the resource wisely. In order to ensure that the resource is conserved, economic planners typically develop a "backup system" for the private market consisting of rules and regulations that constrain the actions of private decision-makers or remove from the private sector all discretion regarding natural resource development. The idea is that if one system (i.e., the market) fails, the backup system (the government) will step in to perform the task. But the value of a redundant system depends on (1) the likelihood of a failure of the primary system, (2) the extent of the damage if the primary system should fail, (3) the cost of the back-stop system, and (4) the effectiveness of government decision-making in its backup role. Unfortunately, these four factors are seldom taken into account by legislators developing public policies toward resources.

By designing a leasing program emphasizing policies that use economic incentives to promote the public interest, the probability of market failure—and its resulting damages—can be minimized and unnecessary costs of government regulation, monitoring, and policing can be avoided.

DATA AND ALGORITHMS USED TO COMPUTE LEASE-SPECIFIC CASH-FLOWS

The principal source of lease-specific data was the USGS Conservation Division's Lease Production and Revenue (LPR) data base. The original computer program to generate lease-specific cash-flows from the LPR data base was developed in 1976 by D. C. Elmendorf of Kappa Systems, Inc., and P. D. Boone of Computer Sciences Corp., under a contract with the USGS. This program was received at the University of California, Santa Barbara, in 1979 and, since then, has been subject to major revisions. In particular, a significant improvement was made when an algorithm was added that allowed estimation of lease-specific tax-payments. Three research projects have been completed at the University of California, Santa Barbara, using the LPR data base but with differing versions of the algorithms for computing lease-specific cash-flows: Mead et al. (1980a,b), Mead et al. (1982), and Muraoka. This Appendix, which is a summary statement of the algorithms used to generate the estimates reported in this volume, is organized into three sections: the first covers cost estimation; the second, production and revenue; and the third, estimation of tax payments.

COST ESTIMATION

For the purpose of estimating costs, detailed studies were made of investment and expenditure patterns for offshore petroleum exploration and development relevant for the area and time period. These studies drew mainly on industry sources of information and published data; the most important of the industry surveys are identified in our footnotes. It was not possible to determine all costs on a lease-specific basis, but the majority of costs, as reflected in the bidding, drilling, rent and royalty payment records contained in the LPR data base, are lease-specific. Still, the cost estimates must be thought of as *averages* for all leases in the relevant category because exploration costs, platform costs, and other costs have been averaged for each year.

Estimates have been made of prelease exploration costs and postlease exploration, drilling, development, and operating costs. At lease shutdown, an estimated abandonment cost was subtracted from the net cash flow of the lease.

Exploration Costs

Exploration costs include all geophysical and geological expenses; seismic, gravity, and magnetic surveys; and costs of geological interpretation and processing. As is true for well drilling, seismic and other geophysical work is usually carried out by independent contractors, not by the major oil companies. About 80 percent of the total acquisition cost of geophysical data is expended in the year following the sale date.

Computer processing and interpretation have risen from about 25 percent of data acquisition costs (1950–1953) to over 100 percent of acquisition costs (since 1975), reflecting improvements in computer technology and increased sophistication of mathematical and other modeling of geological information.

Our exploration cost estimates (Table A-1) are based primarily on data collected and published annually by the Society of Exploration Geophysicists (SEG). These surveys report total crew months, line miles, acquisition costs, processing costs, and rates of change from previous years for offshore seismic and other geophysical effort—in later years targeted to specific offshore locations (Gulf of Mexico, Southern California, Cook Inlet, or Atlantic OCS). Because the quality and specificity of these data vary over the years, we have obtained additional information from seven of the major offshore oil producers. These companies have studied their exploration cost outlays for various time periods (one company for 1954–62, another for 1957–62, etc.). We have used these different company analyses to arrive at exploration cost estimates consistent with the data provided in the SEG reports but expressed in terms of cost per OCS tract acquired.

Table A-1. Exploration Costs—Gulf of Mexico OCS Areas, 1954-1969.

Year*	Cost per Crew Month (Marine Seismic)	Cost of Interpretation & Processing (as % of Data Acquisition Cost)	Total Cost Per Tract Acquired
1954	140,000	30	170,000
1955	145,000	30	170,000
1959	155,000	35	175,000
1960	155,000	35	175,000
1962	165,000	40	180,000
1964	180,000	40	180,000
1966	180,000	30	150,000
1967	120,000	50	140,000
1968	130,000	60	160,000
1969	155,000	60	160,000

SOURCES: Society of Exploration Geophysicists Annual Reports, "Geophysical Activity in 1950-69," *Geophysics,* vols. 17-35, 1951-1970.

Reports from seven major offshore oil producers concerning exploration costs per tract acquired or per acre acquired, 1954-1969.

*Lease sale years only.

The exploration cost estimates reported in Table A-1 apply to all lease sales studied for the years 1954-1969, irrespective of sale type and specific location. Our general approach is supported by the SEG reports and by producers who provided us with data. One of these companies expressed their conclusion most succinctly:

> We do not believe that exploration costs vary to any significant degree due to geographical area, water depth, distance from shore, or whether the sale is wildcat or drainage.

Costs of Drilling and Equipping Wells

Our source of data was the Joint Association Survey of the U.S. Oil and Gas Producing Industry (JAS),[1] which has been issued annually since 1955 (with the exception of the years 1957-58). These surveys contain the most detailed and systematically collected data available on drilling and well equipment costs. The costs of wells in the JAS reports have been

1. Joint Association Survey of the U.S. Oil and Gas Producing Industry. American Petroleum Institute, Washington, D.C. The survey has sections on drilling costs and on expenditures for exploration, development, and production.

classified by year, geographic location, type (oil, gas, or dry), and depth category. Following the JAS classifications, the same four labels were attached to each well drilled on any of the 1,223 leases covered by our study. These labels then define the cost estimate of a particular well.

Two problems with the JAS data made it necessary for us to make adjustments. As mentioned above, surveys are not available for the years 1957–1958. Drilling costs for these years were estimated by interpolation between the 1956 and the 1959 entries. A second problem is that the sample sizes of certain well categories for certain years are very small, and in some cases, some categories have not been sampled at all. Occasionally a small sample size has led to a cost estimate for a well category higher than that for a deeper well in the same category (whether oil, gas, or dry) and year. In such cases, and in cases where no sample existed, we have interpolated between depth categories to overcome the shortcomings of the JAS data. Thus unrealistic estimates were ignored and estimates missing from the JAS data were generated.

The cost elements that respondents to the JAS are asked to include as well-drilling costs are as follows:

> . . . expenditures for drilling dry holes and productive wells and equipping new productive wells through the Christmas tree* installation. More specifically, these cost elements are the costs of labor, materials, supplies, water, fuels, power, and direct overhead (i.e., field, district, and regional), for such operations as site preparation, road building, erecting and dismantling derricks and drilling rigs, drilling holes, running and cementing casing, hauling materials, etc. Include the total cost of water, if purchased, or cost of water well, if drilled and chargeable to oil or gas well-drilling operations. Well costs also include machinery and tool charges and rentals, and depreciation charges, where appropriate, for rigs and other equipment and facilities which will be used in drilling more than one well. Deduct the condition value of materials salvaged after use where appropriate.
>
> For offshore wells, include costs of fixed platforms and islands. Where facilities serve more than one well, the costs should be allocated to each well on the basis of the operator's best current estimate of the ultimate number of wells that will use the facility. Also, include cost expirations (depreciation or amortization) for company-owned mobile platforms, barges, and tenders.

The sum of these cost elements corresponds to the cost category we have labeled "costs of drilling and equipping wells." Because of its length, the set of cost estimates in this category is not reproduced here.

---

*An arrangement of pipes and valves on the casing head. These control the flow of oil and gas.

Algorithm for Drilling and Equipping Costs.   The estimated cost, *C*, of drilling a particular well can be represented by the following general function:

$$C = f(Y,L,D,T,S)$$

where,

Y = the spud year (the year drilling begins), 1954 through 1978; *L* = location, where a distinction is made between offshore Louisiana and other parts of the Gulf of Mexico; *D* = well depth, with eleven depth categories used; *T* = type of lease on which the well was drilled, distinguishing between dry, oil, and gas leases; and *S* = position of well in the calendar drilling sequence. This variable is relevant only if the lease is productive.

The variable *S* requires some additional explanation. Naturally, all wells drilled on a dry lease are considered dry wells. For productive leases, the LPR data base does not identify dry and productive wells. Since the drilling costs as well as other cost elements (to be discussed below) depend on whether a well was dry or not, a general rule is needed to estimate the proportion of productive wells on a productive lease. This problem was solved as follows: For the first eleven wells, 65 percent were assumed to be productive; for the twelfth through the sixteenth wells, 77.5 percent; and for the seventeenth well and beyond, 90 percent. This algorithm is based on, and consistent with, industry experience and USGS data for the number of producing wells on each lease in 1978.

Costs of Equipment Beyond the Christmas Tree for Productive Wells.   The per well costs of equipment beyond the Christmas tree were also estimated, using data from the Joint Association Surveys mentioned in the previous section. The cost estimates in this category are those necessary to convert a drilled well to a producing well. More specifically, they are the costs of artificial and downhole lift equipment, flow lines, flow tanks, separators, and related field facilities.

The costs in this category for any given lease in any given year were set equal to the number of initially productive wells drilled in that year (see *"Algorithm for Drilling and Equipping Costs"* above), times the equipment cost per well (see Table A-2).

Operating Costs for Productive Wells.   Operating costs per well were estimated from JAS data and from our own survey of oil companies. Included were lifting costs and all other costs directly applicable to the production of petroleum, as distinguished from drilling and initial installment of equipment necessary for production. More specifically, the costs in this category are those of labor, field supervision, repair and maintenance, fuel, power, water, small tools, supplies, etc. Operating costs are calculated on the basis of the number of operating wells, with no distinction between oil and gas wells. This approach most closely reflects industry experience. Operating costs in each year were calculated as the number of currently productive wells times an operating cost per well. The number of currently productive wells was calculated as the number of initially productive wells in that year (see *"Algorithm for Drilling and Equipping Costs"* above), plus 96 percent of the producing wells in the preceding year (fractional wells are allowed). Operating costs per currently productive well are shown in Table A–2.

Marginal Overhead Costs.   Overhead expenses relating to bidding, planning, and accounting rise as the activity related to offshore leases acquired by a company rises. We have estimated these marginal overhead costs for each year to be 5 percent of that year's total costs of drilling and equipping wells, costs of equipment beyond the Christmas tree, and operating costs.

Costs of Bonus, Rental, and Royalty.   These costs were taken from the LPR data base. They are derived from USGS historical records. They reflect industry experience exactly, except for minor accounting revisions that sometimes move revenues (royalties) from one year to the next.

Interest Costs.   The current algorithms account for the impact of taxes on lease cash flows. Since interest payments are considered ordinary costs of doing business, these expenses must be estimated and deducted from lease income before computing income taxes. It is necessary to estimate the proportion of total expenses being debt financed, the method for retiring debt over time, and the annual interest rate to be paid on the accumulated debt.

The percentage of total expenses (except taxes) being debt financed is estimated to be 15.6 percent. This estimate is an average for the years 1954–1979 based on information about the composition of assets for a sample of petroleum companies and published in the American Petroleum Institute's *Basic Petroleum Data Book.*[2] The debt percentage for the companies in the sample has been relatively stable over that period of time.

Debt is assumed to be retired over the lifetime of leases. The amount of debt retired in a specific year is equal to 10 percent of the consolidated debt in that year. Debt remaining at the time of abandonment is assumed to be paid in the abandonment year.

The estimated interest payment in a year is equal to the consolidated

---

2. The American Petroleum Institute, *Basic Petroleum Data Book,* vol. 1, no. 2, section 5, table 3 (Washington, D.C.: The American Petroleum Institute, May 1981).

Table A–2. Cost per Well for Equipment Beyond the Christmas Tree for Initially Productive Wells and Operating Cost per Currently Productive Well.

Year	Cost of Equipment Beyond the Christmas Tree	Operating Cost*
1954	$60,547	$35,000
1955	60,547	35,000
1956	60,764	35,000
1957	62,443	35,000
1958	64,121	35,000
1959	64,800	35,000
1960	65,423	35,000
1961	64,610	35,000
1962	61,775	35,000
1963	62,958	35,000
1964	62,622	38,000
1965	70,286	38,000
1966	78,962	38,000
1967	77,163	40,000
1968	81,889	40,000
1969	95,321	41,000
1970	96,260	42,000
1971	103,961	42,000
1972	114,724	54,000
1973	115,830	60,000
1974	140,303	70,000
1975	180,433	90,000
1976	211,670	90,000
1977	226,232	97,200
1978	246,426	104,295
1979	**	113,056
1980	**	122,892

SOURCE: Data Resources, Inc., *U.S. Long Term Review,* Summer 1981.

*Operating costs have been estimated for the years 1981–2010 by multiplying the 1980 entry by the forecasted index of hourly wage rates.
**Not applicable.

debt in that year times the rate charged on long-term, triple A bonds.[3]

Costs of Abandonment. Abandonment represents a relatively new component of costs for oil companies operating in OCS areas. Before

3. For the historical period (1954–1980), the data on the long-term triple A bond rate have been obtained from the *Economic Report of the President* (various issues). For the future period, the estimates in Data Resources, Inc., *U.S. Long Term Review* (Summer 1981) have been used.

1970, only a few very old, shallow-water platforms had been abandoned.[4] In these cases, the salvage value of equipment and materials was approximately equal to the removal and dismantling costs, producing no net cost.

In recent years there has been a rapid increase in net abandonment costs resulting from the combination of stricter environmental regulations affecting abandonment, platform installations in deeper water (with greater numbers and strength of pilings), and reductions in the relative scrap values of equipment and materials salvaged from abandoned tracts. Since oil companies currently expect that platform abandonment will impose a future cost approximately equal to current installation cost, they are taking these future costs into account in developing bonus bids for OCS tracts.

We have obtained information on abandonment costs from three major oil companies. In two cases, these data are confidential; in the third, the data have been supplied as part of the Federal Energy Regulatory Commission's public record.[5]

Net-of-salvage cost estimates for abandonment are shown in Table A-3. These estimates incorporate the known costs of 1977–78 abandonments and the assumption that net abandonment costs in the period prior to 1970 were close to zero.

The LPR data base contains information on leases terminated prior to 1980. For these leases, abandonment costs (as shown in Table A-3) were subtracted from the lease cash flow in the year of termination. The abandonment decision for leases in effect in 1979 was simulated as follows: The after-tax present value (including abandonment costs) was computed conditional on abandonment for each of the years 1980–2010, using the long-term, triple A bond rate as the discount rate. The selected year of abandonment was that which maximized the present value of the lease.

OUTPUT AND REVENUE

Annual Revenue for the Historical Period

Lease gross revenue for years from lease sale through 1979 equals actual royalty payments, as recorded in the LPR data base, times 6.

---

4. For the 839 leases issued in the Gulf of Mexico between 1954 and 1962, the record indicates that only fifteen tracts had been relinquished, with associated abandonment of platforms, through 1976.

5. FERC Docket Nos. CI77-702, CI78-96, CI78-498 through 503, and CI78-767, August 1978.

Table A-3. Estimated Costs of Abandonment, Gulf of Mexico OCS.

Year*	Net Fixed Cost Per OCS Tract ($M)	Additional Variable Cost per Well ($M)
1967	0	0
1968	50	10
1969	100	20
1970	150	30
1971	200	40
1972	250	50
1973	300	60
1974	350	70
1975	400	80
1976	450	90
1977	500	100
1978	537	107
1979	582	116
1980	632	126

Source: Data Resources, Inc., *U.S. Long Term Review,* Summer (1980).

*Abandonment costs for the years 1981–2010 were generated by multiplying the 1980 entry by the forecasted index of hourly wage rates 1981–2010.

Annual Revenue for the Future Period

Future gross revenue was computed as the product of predicted future production (see "Future Production" below), times predicted future prices net of windfall profits taxes on oil (see "Future Prices—Crude Oil Price Forecast" below).

Future Production

A constant exponential decline rate was used to predict future levels of output for liquids (oil plus condensate), gas, and other hydrocarbons (classified as "other"). Under this method

$$Q_i = Q_{i-1} \cdot e^{-d}$$

where Q is the quantity in question subscripted by reference to a particular year; i may range from 1979 to 2010; e is the base of the natural logarithmic system; and d is the decline rate.

The decline rate of 0.15 applied in our IRR analysis was selected by observing decline rates for a sample of leases issued early in the period under study (the peak production of leases in the sample occurred within the period in which historical information on production levels is available). This rate was found to be appropriate in describing production declines for the leases in the sample.

Future Prices—Natural Gas Price Forecast

The Natural Gas Policy Act of 1978 provided for decontrol of "new gas" from the Outer Continental Shelf by January 1, 1985, but it required continued controls over "old gas." Since all leases under study were issued prior to April 20, 1977, their gas production is subject to permanent price control.

The act provides for separate treatment of old gas supplied under a contract in existence in 1977, and of old gas supplied under a contract entered into after 1977 and thus replacing an expired contract. The former is referred to as a non-rollover contract and the latter as a rollover contract.

For non-rollover gas, the "maximum lawful price" for old gas is "the just and reasonable rate" established by the Federal Energy Regulatory Commission (FERC), multiplied by an inflation factor, specified as the U.S. Department of Commerce GNP implicit price deflator. This maximum may be inoperative if existing contracts call for a lower price.

For rollover gas, the act provides for the higher of (1) the price of non-rollover gas, or (2) $0.54 per million BTUs for April 1977, multiplied by the inflation adjustment factor based on the same date.

We have no way of knowing what the FERC will determine to be the "just and reasonable rate" for the future. Lease-specific gas prices in the years 1977–1979 are of little help, since they reflect prices for gas committed to sales over many years (beginning with first production in 1959) and include new sales contracts every year.

For the non-rollover gas, we begin with a 1979 price equal to the actual price by lease.[6] This price is multiplied by a GNP deflator forecast for the period 1980–2010 to generate the non-rollover gas price forecast for that period.[7]

For rollover gas, it is arbitrarily assumed that 50 percent is priced at the FERC "just and reasonable" price, set equal to $1/Mcf in 1977. The

6. The 1979 lease-specific gas price used as a forecasting base is constrained to a minimum of 20c/Mcf and a maximum of $3/Mcf to eliminate illogically low or high average gas prices resulting from USGS accounting corrections made on some leases each year.

7. The GNP implicit price forecast used for the period 1981–2010 is taken from Data Resources, Inc., *U.S. Long Term Review* (Summer 1981).

remaining 50 percent is assumed to be priced at 54c/Mcf in 1977. The average of these two prices is 77 cents. This estimated average price of rollover gas is subject to price escalation by the GNP deflator and becomes 97 cents in 1980. For the period 1980–2010, it is subject to escalation by the GNP deflator forecast.

Since we have no data on the magnitude of probable volumes of gas covered by the rollover provision, we will assume a straight line relationship from zero rollover volume in 1979 to 100 percent of total production in 2010.

With the base price of gas in 1977 set below $1/Mcf, and price escalation limited to the GNP deflator, the only possibilities for natural gas prices rising to market clearing levels would be (1) for the price of crude oil to fall sharply, or (2) for the FERC to substantially increase the price of natural gas under its "just and reasonable" authority. Neither event appears to be likely. Therefore, price controls are expected to hold the wellhead price of natural gas below market clearing levels for as long as old gas is produced from the OCS.

Future Price—Crude Oil Price Forecast

The future price forecast for crude oil is derived from Data Resources, Inc., *U.S. Long Term Review* (Summer 1981).[8] This forecast allows for an increase in the price of crude oil to producers of 49.5 percent in 1981 and annual increases in range 8.2 percent to 12.8 percent in the years thereafter. The price forecast, however, does not take into account the effect of the Crude Oil Windfall Profit Tax Act of 1980 on the net price received by the producer. The windfall profit tax is applied to the windfall tax base, defined as the difference between the actual selling price of crude oil and a base price set by federal regulations. It should therefore more properly be thought of as an excise tax.[9]

The provisions of the Windfall Profit Tax as enacted are incorporated in the analysis. All production from the 1954–1969 leases is classified as old oil, and all lessees are large companies, according to tax definitions. The applicable tax rate is therefore 70 percent of the windfall tax base. The windfall tax became effective in 1980 and is scheduled to begin phase-out not earlier than 1988 or later than 1991. When the phase-out

---

8. The forecasted crude oil price is U.S. Refiners' Acquisition Price for Domestic Crude Oil.

9. The act limits total tax liability to 90 percent of net income from the oil and gas producing property. But in this case, the computation of net income does not allow treatment of percentage depletion, intangible drilling costs, and windfall profit tax as expenses. This "90 percent of net" rule is built into our computational algorithm.

begins, the tax liability of each producer will be reduced by 3 percent per month for 33 months. In our analysis, we conservatively assume that the phase-out will commence in 1991 and will be completed by the end of 1993. The net future price of crude oil to the producer is determined by subtracting the per barrel windfall tax from the world market price, as given by the following equation:

$$Pp = MP - [(MP - BP) \times .70]$$

where,

P_p = price of crude oil to the producer, MP = market price of crude oil, and BP = base price of crude oil.

The approximate initial base price of OCS oil produced in the quarter beginning March 1, 1980, is $12.81.[10] The base price is escalated quarterly in accordance with the percentage change in the GNP deflator from the second quarter of 1979. The adjustment process is lagged two quarters.

TAX EXPENDITURES

The annual tax liability attributable to a lease was estimated as described below and subtracted from the lease cash flow. Because of limitations on data availability, some simplifying assumptions were necessary.

The LPR data base records production and revenue by calendar year. Estimates of tax payments are therefore also by calendar year and not by fiscal year. Changes in relevant tax statutes effective between January and December are treated as applicable to the entire year, unless otherwise stated. We further assume that all OCS lessee firms have sufficient income or tax liabilities from non-OCS sources to fully utilize any tax advantage that results from OCS activity. And last, long-term capital gains that companies can realize by selling lease rights are not accounted for, since we have no data on such transactions.[11]

The following aspects of oil and gas industry taxation are discussed below: (1) expensing of intangible drilling costs and dry hole costs,

10. The base price of tier-one oil (applicable to the OCS) is the May 1979 upper tier ceiling price as set by the Department of Energy regulations less $0.21. The $12.81 figure given above is the average base price of tier-one oil as estimated in Prentice Hall, Inc., "A Concise Explanation of the Crude Oil Windfall Profit Tax Act of 1980."

11. Muraoka (in his unpublished doctoral dissertation, UC Santa Barbara, 1981, pp. 111–22) has estimated the impact of the favorable tax treatment of long-term capital gains. His computational procedure assumes that the lessee sells his lease rights in a given year if the after-tax value of selling it exceeds the after-tax value of retaining the lease. Muraoka's sample consisted of all the leases issued for the Gulf of Mexico over the years 1954–1969. He found that the aggregate after-tax internal rate of return increases from 11.37 percent to 11.71 percent, if capital gains are accounted for (see p. 121).

(2) depreciation of tangible drilling costs, (3) investment tax credit, (4) percentage and cost depletion, (5) minimum tax, and (6) corporate income tax rates.

Tax Treatment of Drilling Costs

The term *drilling costs,* as used in this section, comprises the costs of drilling and equipping wells and, for productive leases, the cost of equipment beyond the Christmas tree installation.

For the purpose of computing taxes, the costs of dry wells are expensed in the year in which they are incurred. All wells drilled on leases with no production record are treated as dry hole costs and thus expensed in the year drilling commences. Dry wells on productive leases are treated similarly.[12]

For productive wells, drilling costs are divisible into two categories. The first category, intangible costs, are expensed as they are incurred.

> [They] include costs of labor, fuel, power, materials, supplies, tool rental, and repair of drilling equipment. They typically account for about 75 percent of the costs of drilling productive wells. The remaining costs of drilling such wells, called tangible drilling costs, include expenditures for pipe, pumps, tanks and other equipment. The latter must be recovered through depreciation allowances.[13]

Our algorithm assumes that 74.3 percent of total drilling costs are expensed. This estimate is an average for the sample of offshore Louisiana wells included in the JAS data in the years 1955–1964.[14]

The remaining 25.7 percent of drilling costs (the tangible portion) must be capitalized. These costs are recovered by the firm through depreciation. The tax treatment of tangible drilling costs does not differ from the tax treatment of tangible assets in other industries.

Since 1954, depreciation guidelines have been liberalized. In particular, the period of time over which an asset can be fully depreciated, referred to as an asset's useful life, has been shortened. We assume that capitalized assets used on the OCS are depreciated over a twelve-year

12. The procedure for distinguishing between dry and productive wells on producing leases was described in an earlier section of this appendix entitled "Algorithm for Drilling and Equipping Costs."

13. S. L. McDonald, "Taxation System and Market Distortion," in R. J. Kalter and W. A. Vogely, eds., *Energy Supply and Government Policy* (Ithaca, N.Y.: Cornell University Press, 1976), p. 29.

14. The Joint Association surveys published after 1964 do not report the relative shares of intangible and tangible drilling costs.

useful life, and we employ the double declining balance method of accelerated depreciation. If any amount remains in the depreciation account at the time of abandonment, it is written off in that year.

A twelve-year useful life is within the range of allowable depreciation periods for equipment used in Marine Contract Construction (asset guideline class 15.2). This category includes oil platforms and support vessels. Such equipment can be depreciated in as few as nine-and-a-half years or in as many as fourteen-and-a-half years. A twelve-year useful life is the mean value for marine contract equipment.

Investment Tax Credit

The investment tax credit was first initiated during the Kennedy administration in 1962. It provides a credit against the corporate tax liability equal to a percentage of qualified investments made by the firm. The allowed credit rate depends upon the type of investment.

We assume that all tangible assets used on the OCS are new and have a useful life in excess of seven years. The total cost of such assets is thus deemed "qualified investment." The maximum credit rate is allowed for assets so classified.

In our algorithm, the basis for the investment tax credit is the tangible drilling costs. The investment credit rate for any given year is the allowed percentage credit for that year multiplied by the fraction of the days in that year for which the credit is in effect. These percentages are given in Table A–4.

Table A–4. Percentage of Investment Taken as Credit.

Year	% of Investment
1954–61	0
1962–65	7.00
1966	5.41
1967	5.70
1968	7.00
1969	1.88
1970	0
1971	2.65
1972–74	7.00
1975	9.82
1976–after	10.00

Percentage and Cost Depletion

The consumption of capital in the process of production is a cost to the firm. Firms are allowed to deduct this cost, in the form of depreciation, in arriving at taxable income. Depletion for mineral assets is analogous to ordinary depreciation in that it represents the wasting of an asset as production proceeds.

There are two methods of computing the depletion deduction: percentage depletion and cost depletion. The tax advantages of percentage depletion were eliminated for all integrated oil companies in 1975. Until 1975, OCS lessees were permitted to deduct from gross income the larger of the amounts obtained by use of each method—percentage depletion or the more conventional cost depletion.

Cost depletion is computed in the following fashion: The total production from a given lease in the current tax period is divided by the total production from the lease over its remaining life—as determined by the actual production profile of each lease, including the estimated future production through the shutdown year.[15] This ratio is in turn multiplied by the remaining capitalized basis of the property to determine the cost depletion allowed in the current period. The "remaining capitalized basis" is the initial capitalized value of the bonus payment and the prelease exploration costs less prior depletion deductions. If the basis has previously been depleted to zero, then no cost depletion is allowed.[16] This formulation of cost depletion has been in use since 1954. It is important to note that a firm can use cost depletion one year and percentage depletion in future years, if percentage depletion provides a larger deduction.

Percentage depletion is an alternative method, allowed to major oil companies through 1974, for calculating the depletion deduction. The computation of percentage depletion is as follows:

Gross income from each lease is multiplied by a given percentage depletion rate, 27.5 percent in 1954–1969, 22 percent in 1970–1974, and

---

15. In the likely event that oil and gas are both produced from a given tract, the taxpayer can convert gas production into oil equivalents and compute the depletion deduction on that basis.

16. Our estimate of cost depletion will differ from the computation made by each lessee who is permitted to revise estimates of the total quantity of recoverable reserves annually as information about the geological structure becomes known. It is not clear whether lessees have consistently under- or overestimated the ultimate reserves from OCS leases in determining cost depletion deductions. To the extent that they have underestimated such reserves, their early cost depletion deductions will exceed those arrived at by our formula.

zero thereafter.[17] The resulting percentage depletion deduction is subject to an upper limit of 50 percent of the *net* income from the lease. Net income is defined as gross income less all costs attributable to the lease except depletion.

The percentage depletion allowance is calculated for each lease individually. If percentage depletion, rather than cost depletion, is claimed, the basis of the capitalized bonus and prelease exploration cost is reduced by the amount of the percentage depletion allowance. Note that the sum of percentage depletion deductions over the life of a productive lease may (and usually will) exceed the initial capital investment. This feature distinguishes percentage depletion from cost depletion and ordinary depreciation, which are limited to the initial value of the investment. Beginning in 1970, the tax advantages of percentage depletion were reduced by the minimum tax, as explained in the next section.

Minimum Tax

Since 1970, corporate taxpayers have been required to pay an additional tax on a base comprised of items that receive preferential tax treatment. For OCS production, the relevant preference items are percentage depletion and long-term capital gains. In our analysis, the latter item does not increase estimated tax liabilities because of the assumption that lease properties have not changed hands during their productive lives. However, in a year in which percentage depletion is claimed, the difference between the percentage depletion taken and the cost depletion that would have been allowed otherwise is considered preference income and is added to the minimum tax base.

From 1970 through 1974 the minimum tax was calculated as 10 percent of the adjusted minimum tax base. The adjusted base is composed of the tax preference items listed above less (1) $30,000 and (2) the tax liability of the taxpayer, plus (3) the investment credit claimed by the taxpayer.

To account for the impact of the minimum tax on the tax liability of OCS firms, we adopt Brannon's estimate that in its first year (1970) the minimum tax had the net effect of reducing the statutory percentage depletion rate by 2 percent.[18] The minimum tax need only be considered from

17. Gross income for depletion purposes is equal to gross revenue less royalty payments and bonus amortization.

18. G. M. Brannon, "Existing Tax Differentials and Subsidies Relating to the Energy Industries," in G. M. Brannon, ed., *Studies in Energy Tax Policy* (Cambridge, Mass.: Ballinger Publishing Co., 1975), p. 5.

1970 through 1974. Thus to approximate the impact of the minimum tax, the percentage depletion rate is reduced from 22 percent to 20 percent from 1970 to 1974. After that time, OCS lessee firms are no longer able to utilize percentage depletion and will therefore have no preference tax base.

Corporate Income Tax Rates

The rate and structure of the corporate income tax has changed significantly from 1954 to the present. The current rate structure is progressive. Thus the marginal tax rate (the amount of tax paid on the last dollar of taxable income) increases as the level of taxable income increases. Since OCS lessees are relatively large firms, we assume that all income derived from OCS production is subject to the maximum marginal corporate tax rate. The corporate tax liability attributable to a particular OCS lease is therefore the product of the taxable income derived from that lease and the applicable marginal tax rate. Taxable income is defined as the gross income from the lease less royalty payments, production costs, and all other legal deductions. These deductions include cost or percentage depletion, expensing of intangible drilling costs, depreciation of tangible drilling costs, expensing of dry hole costs, expensing of lease abandonment costs, the windfall profits tax, and various state taxes.

The maximum marginal corporate tax rate was 52 percent in 1954–1963, 50 percent in 1964, 48 percent in 1965–1978, and 46 percent thereafter.

From 1968 through 1970, corporations were required to pay a surcharge in addition to the corporate income tax. The surcharge was computed as a percentage of the regular corporate tax, 10 percent in 1968–1969, and 2.5 percent in 1970.

We account for the corporate surcharge by altering the maximum marginal tax rate in the relevant years. Thus converted, the 48 percent regular tax rate becomes an effective tax rate of 52.8 percent in 1968 and 1969, and 49.2 percent in 1970.

OCS oil and gas production does not come under the taxing jurisdiction of any state and therefore is not subject to state severance taxes. Nevertheless, additional income generated by OCS activities may generate additional state tax liabilities under unitary state tax formulas. Unitary formulas, which vary from one state to another, are used by many states to determine the portion of worldwide corporate income of a multistate business that is taxable by the state.

Estimating the impact of state unitary taxes requires state-by-state financial information on each OCS firm. We lack the data needed to estimate state unitary taxes directly; thus, the effect of these taxes is accommodated by adding 2 percent to the federal corporate tax rate each year. This estimate is based upon the experience of major oil companies having operations in unitary tax states. It includes allowance for the deduction of state tax obligations from federal taxes.

Summary of Algorithm for Computing Taxes

Table A–5 summarizes our interpretation of relevant tax statutes. Effective tax rates, tax credit rates, and percentage depletion rates used in this study are summarized in Table A–6. Effective rates may vary from statutory rates because of the interaction of several tax principles. For example, the minimum tax is accommodated by adjusting the percentage depletion rate, while the income tax surcharge and state corporate taxes are handled by adjusting the corporate tax rate. If a tax or credit is in effect for only a portion of a year, the effective rate is determined by multiplying the statutory rate by the percentage of days in the year the rate was in effect. This method is used for both the investment tax credit and the windfall profits tax.

Table A–5. Tax Treatment of OCS Oil and Gas Lease Costs.

Type of Cost	*Tax Treatment*
1. Bonus and prelease exploration costs	1. Capitalized
a. Lease proves productive	a. Recovered through depletion
b. Lease proves unproductive	b. Charged off as loss on surrender of lease
2. Lease rentals	2. Expensed as incurred
3. Dry hole costs	3. Expensed as incurred
4. Intangible costs of productive wells	4. Expensed as incurred
5. Tangible equipment on productive wells	5. Capitalized and recovered through depreciation
6. Royalties	6. Expensed as incurred
7. Production costs	7. Expensed as incurred
8. Abandonment costs	8. Expensed as incurred

Source: Derived from S. L. McDonald, *Federal Tax Treatment of Income from Oil and Gas* (Washington, D.C.: The Brookings Institution, 1963), p. 17.

Table A–6. Effective Tax, Credit, and Deduction Rates From 1954.

Year	Effective Corporate Tax Rate	Effective Depletion Rate	Effective Investment Tax Credit Rate	Effective Windfall Profit Tax Rate
	(%)	(%)	(%)	(%)
1954–61	54.0	27.5	–	–
1962–63	54.0	27.5	7.00	–
1964	52.0	27.5	7.00	–
1965	50.0	27.5	7.00	–
1966	50.0	27.5	5.41	–
1967	50.0	27.5	5.70	–
1968	54.8	27.5	7.00	–
1969	54.8	27.5	1.88	–
1970	51.2	20.0	–	–
1971	50.0	20.0	2.65	–
1972–74	50.0	20.0	7.00	–
1975	50.0	–	9.82	–
1976–78	50.0	–	10.00	–
1979	48.0	–	10.00	–
1980	48.0	–	10.00	58.68
1981–90	48.0	–	10.00	70.00
1991	48.0	–	10.00	56.35
1992	48.0	–	10.00	31.15
1993	48.0	–	10.00	6.83
1994–	48.0	–	10.00	–

SOURCE: W. J. Mead, D. D. Muraoka, and P. E. Sorensen, "The Effect of Taxes on the Profitability of U.S. Oil and Gas Production: A Case Study of the OCS Record," *National Tax Journal* 35 (no. 1, March 1982):26.

SELECTED BIBLIOGRAPHY

Agria, S. R. "Special Tax Treatment of Mineral Industries." In A. C. Harberger and M. J. Baily, eds., *The Taxation of Income from Capital*. Washington, D.C.: The Brookings Institution, 1969.

Anderson, Arthur and Company. *Oil and Gas Federal Income Tax Manual*, 8th ed. Chicago, 1960.

American Petroleum Institute. *Basic Petroleum Data Book*, vol. 1, no. 4. Washington, D.C., May 1981.

———. *Joint Association Survey of the U.S. Oil and Gas Producing Industry*. Washington, D.C., various issues.

Baumol, W. J. "Contestable Markets: An Uprising in the Theory of Industry Structure." *American Economic Review* 72 (March 1982):1-15.

Brannon, G. M. "Existing Tax Differentials and Subsidies Relating to the Energy Industries." In G. M. Brannon, ed., *Studies in Energy Tax Policy*. Cambridge, Mass.: Ballinger Publishing Co., 1975.

Brannon, G. M., ed. *Energy Taxes and Subsidies*. Cambridge, Mass.: Ballinger Publishing Co., 1975.

Capen, E. C.; R. V. Clapp; and W. M. Cambell. "Competitive Bidding in High Risk Situations." *Journal of Petroleum Technology* 23:641-53.

Coase, R. "The Problem of Social Cost." *Journal of Law and Economics* 3 (Oct. 1960):1-44.

Commerce Clearing House. "Explanation of the Crude Oil Windfall Profit Tax Act of 1980." *Federal Tax Guide Reports*, no. 27, vol. 63. Chicago: Commerce Clearing House, 1980.

——. *Federal Tax Guide*. Chicago: Commerce Clearing House, updated continuously.

Dam, K. W. *Oil Resources*. Chicago: University of Chicago Press, 1976.

Data Resources, Inc. *U.S. Long Term Review*. Lexington, Mass., Summer 1981.

Dougherty, E. L., and J. Lohrenz. "Statistical Analysis for Solo and Joint Bids for Federal Offshore Oil and Gas Leases." Paper presented at meeting of Society of Petroleum Engineers, Bakersfield, Calif., April 13–15, 1977.

Dougherty, E. L., and M. Nozaki. "Determining Optimum Bid Fraction." *Journal of Petroleum Technology* 27 (1975):349–56.

Engelbrect-Wiggans, R. "Auctions and Bidding Models: A Survey." *Management Science* 26 (no. 2, Feb. 1980):119–42.

Gaskins, D. W., and B. Vann. "Joint Buying and the Seller's Return—The Case of OCS Leases." In *Energy Industry Investigations*, Part 1, Hearings before the Subcommittee on Monopolies and Commercial Law, House Judicial Committee, 94th Congress, 1979.

Gilley, O. W., and G. V. Karels. "The Competitive Effect in Bonus Bidding: New Evidence." *Bell Journal of Economics* 12 (no. 2, Autumn 1981):637–48.

Gordon, R. L. "A Reinterpretation of the Pure Theory of Exhaustion." *Journal of Political Economy* 75 (no. 3, June 1967):274–86.

Gray, L. C. "Rent Under the Assumption of Exhaustibility." *Quarterly Journal of Economics* 28 (May 1914):66–89.

Gwartney, J., and R. Stroup. *Economics: Private and Public Choice*. Orlando, Fla.: Academic Press, 1983.

Herfindahl, O. C. "Depletion and Economic Theory." In M. Gaffney, ed., *Extractive Resources and Taxation*, pp. 63–90. Madison: University of Wisconsin Press, 1967.

Hotelling, H. "The Economics of Exhaustible Resources." *Journal of Political Economy* 39 (no. 2, April 1931):137–75.

Internal Revenue Service. *Statement of Income, Corporate Income Tax Returns*, Publication No. 16. Washington, D.C.: U.S. Government Printing Office, 1954 to 1976 editions.

Jones, R. O.; W. J. Mead; and P. E. Sorensen. "Economic Issues in Oil Shale Leasing Policy." *Eleventh Oil Shale Symposium Proceedings*, pp. 203–13. Golden: Colorado School of Mines, 1978.

——. "The Outer Continental Shelf Lands Act Amendments of 1978." *Natural Resources Journal* 19 (Oct. 1979):885–908.

——. "Free Entry Into Crude Oil and Gas Production and Competition in the U.S. Oil Industry." In W. J. Mead and A. E. Utton, eds., *U.S. Energy Policy: Errors of the Past, Proposals for the Future*, pp. 157–74. Cambridge, Mass.: Ballinger Publishing Co., 1979.

——. "Do Bidders in OCS Oil and Gas Lease Sales Behave Rationally?" In J. Dunkerly, ed., *International Energy Strategies*. Cambridge, Mass.: Oelgeschlager, Gunn & Hain, 1980.

Leland, H. L. "Optimal Risk Sharing and the Leasing of Natural Resources,

With Applications to Oil and Gas Leasing on the OCS." *Quarterly Journal of Economics* 92 (Aug. 1978):413–37.

Markham, J. W. "The Competitive Effects of Joint Bidding by Oil Companies for Offshore Leases." In J. W. Markham and G. F. Papanek, eds., *Industrial Organization and Economic Development*, pp. 116–35. Boston: Houghton Mifflin Co., 1970.

McDonald, S. L. *Federal Tax Treatment of Income From Oil and Gas*. Washington, D.C.: The Brookings Institution, 1963.

———. *Petroleum Conservation in the United States: An Economic Analysis*. Baltimore: Johns Hopkins University Press for Resources for the Future, 1971.

———. "Taxation System and Market Distortion." In R. J. Kalter and W. A. Vogely, eds., *Energy Supply and Government Policy*. Ithaca, N.Y.: Cornell University Press, 1976.

———. *The Leasing of Federal Lands for Fossil Fuel Production*. Baltimore: Johns Hopkins University Press for Resources for the Future, 1979.

———. "Federal Energy Resource Leasing Policy." In W. J. Mead and A. E. Utton, eds., *U.S. Energy Policy: Errors of the Past, Proposals for the Future*, pp. 45–58. Cambridge, Mass.: Ballinger Publishing Co., 1979.

Mead, W. J. "Natural Resource Disposal Policy—Oral Versus Sealed Bidding." *Natural Resources Journal* 7 (April 1967):194–224.

———. "Federal Public Lands Leasing Policies." *Colorado School of Mines Quarterly* 64 (Oct. 1969):181–214.

———. "Cash Bonus Bidding for Mineral Resources." In M. Crommelin and A. R. Thompson, eds., *Mineral Leasing as an Instrument of Public Policy*, pp. 46–56. Vancouver: University of British Columbia Press for the British Institute for Economic Policy Analysis, 1977.

———. "The Rate of Return Earned by Lessees Under Cash Bonus Bidding for OCS Oil and Gas Leases." *Energy Journal* 4 (no. 4, 1983):37–52.

———. "Efficiency in Leasing." In Paul Tempest, ed., *International Energy Markets*, pp. 85–92. Cambridge, Mass.: Oelgeschlager, Gunn & Hain, 1983.

Mead, W. J., and G. G. Pickett. "An Economic Analysis of Oil and Gas Leasing Experience Under Profit-Share and Bonus Bidding With a Fixed Royalty." In M. Neiman and B. Burt, eds., *The Social Constraints on Energy—Policy Implementation*, pp. 39–61. Lexington, Mass.: Lexington Books, 1983.

———. "Federal Leasing Policy." In S. F. Singer, ed., *Free Market Energy, the Way to Benefit Consumers*, pp. 189–217. New York: Universe Books, 1984.

Mead, W. J.; A. Moseidjord; and D. D. Muraoka. "Alternative Bid Variables as Instruments of OCS Leasing Policy." *Contemporary Policy Issues* 1 (no. 5, March 1984):30–43.

Mead, W. J.; A. Moseidjord; and P. E. Sorensen. "The Rate of Return Earned by Lessees Under Cash Bonus Bidding for OCS Oil and Gas Leases." *Energy Journal* 4 (no. 4, 1983):37–52.

———. "Efficiency in Leasing." In Paul Tempest, ed., *International Energy*

Markets, pp. 85–92. Cambridge, Mass.: Oelgeschlager, Gunn & Hain, 1983.

———. "Competition in OCS Oil and Gas Lease Auctions—A Statistical Analysis of Winning Bids." *Natural Resources Journal*, forthcoming, January 1986.

———. *Competitive Bidding Under Asymmetric Information*, Final Report, USGS Contract No. 14-08-0001-18678, 31 Jan. 1982.

———. "Competitive Bidding Under Asymmetrical Information: Behavior and Performance in Gulf of Mexico Drainage Lease Sales, 1959–1969." *Review of Economics and Statistics* 66 (no. 3):505–8.

Mead, W. J., and D. D. Muraoka. "Sensitivity of Rates of Return and Output to Alternative Tax Regimes: The Case of the U.S. Gulf of Mexico OCS." *Energy Journal*, forthcoming.

Mead, W. J.; D. D. Muraoka; and P. E. Sorensen. "The Effect of Taxes on the Profitability of U.S. Oil and Gas Production: A Case Study of the OCS Record." *National Tax Journal* 35 (1982):21–29.

———. "The Economic Impacts of Differential Tax Treatment of Income Derived From Oil and Gas." *Oil and Gas Tax Quarterly* 31 (no. 4, June 1983):895–910.

Mead, W. J.; M. Schniepp; and R. B. Watson. *The Effectiveness of Competition and Appraisals in the Auction Markets for National Forest Timber in the Pacific Northwest*. USFS Contract No. 53-3187-1-43 and PSW G-34, 30 Sept. 1981.

Mead, W. J., and P. E. Sorensen. "The Economic Cost of the Santa Barbara Oil Spill." In *Santa Barbara Oil Spill: An Environmental Inquiry*. University of California at Santa Barbara, California Marine Science Institute, Santa Barbara, 1972.

Mead, W. J.; P. E. Sorensen; R. O. Jones; and A. Moseidjord. *Competition and Performance in OCS Oil and Gas Lease Sales and Lease Development, 1954–1969*. Final Report, USGS Contract No. 14-08-0001-16552, 1 March 1980.

Mead, W. J.; P. E. Sorensen; A. Moseidjord; and D. D. Muraoka. *Additional Studies of Competition and Performance in OCS Oil and Gas Sales, 1954–1975*. Final Report, USGS Contract No. 14-08-0001-18678, 30 Nov. 1980.

Miller, E. "Some Implications of Land Ownership Patterns for Petroleum Policy." *Land Economics* 49 (Nov. 1973):414–23.

Miller, K. G. *Oil and Gas Federal Income Taxation*, 3rd ed. Chicago: Commerce Clearing House, 1957.

Millsaps, S. W., and M. Ott. "Information and Bidding Behavior by Major Oil Companies for Outer Continental Shelf Leases: Is the Joint Bidding Ban Justified?" *Energy Journal* 2 (no. 3, July 1981):71–90.

Moffet, W. R. "Federal Energy Proprietorship: Leasing and Its Critics." In *Options for U.S. Energy Policy*, pp. 211–35. San Francisco: Institute for Contemporary Studies, 1977.

Moseidjord, A. *Competitive Bidding Under Asymmetric Information*. Ph.D. dissertation, University of California, Santa Barbara, 1981.

Moseidjord, A., and D. D. Muraoka. "Managing the Risk of Outer Continental Shelf Oil and Gas Leases." In M. H. Hamza, ed., *Proceedings of the IASTED International Symposium on Energy, Power and Environmental Systems, San Francisco, June 4–6, 1984*, pp. 9–11. Anaheim, Calif.: Acta Press, 1984.

Muraoka, D. D. "The Effect of Taxation on the Rate of Return on Outer Continental Shelf Leases Issued from 1954 to 1969." Unpublished Ph.D. dissertation, University of California, Santa Barbara, 1981.

Muraoka, D. D., and R. B. Watson. "Economic Issues in Federal Timber Sale Procedures." In R. T. Deacon and M. B. Johnson, eds., *Forestlands: Public and Private*. San Francisco: Pacific Institute for Public Policy Research, 1985.

Pasztor, A. "Reagan Moving Toward Giving States Larger Share of Offshore Leasing Money." *Wall Street Journal*, 13 June 1984, p. 15.

Peterson, F. M. "The Government Role in Mineral Exploration." In M. Crommelin and A. R. Thompson, eds., *Mineral Leasing as an Instrument of Public Policy*. Vancouver: University of British Columbia Press for the British Institute for Economic Policy Analysis, 1977.

———. "Two Externalities in Petroleum Exploration." In G. M. Brannon, ed., *Studies in Energy Tax Policy*, pp. 101–13. Cambridge, Mass.: Ballinger Publishing Co., 1975.

Pickett, G. G. "An Option Valuation Model of Bonus Bidding and Profit-Share Bidding for Offshore Oil and Gas Leases." Unpublished Ph.D. dissertation, University of California at Santa Barbara, 1983.

Prentice-Hall, Inc. "A Concise Explanation of the Crude Oil Windfall Profit Tax of 1980." *Prentice-Hall Federal Taxes*, Report Bulletin 17, vol. 61, sec. 2. Englewood Cliffs, N.J.: Prentice-Hall, Inc., 2 April 1980.

Ramsey, J. B. *Bidding and Oil Leases*, Contemporary Studies in Economic and Financial Analysis, vol. 25. Greenwich, Conn.: FAI Press, 1980.

Reece, D. K. "Competitive Bidding for Offshore Petroleum Resources." *Bell Journal of Economics* 9 (no. 2, Autumn 1979):169–84.

Scott, A. "The Theory of the Mine Under Conditions of Certainty." In M. Gaffney, ed., *Extractive Resources and Taxation*, pp. 25–62. Madison: University of Wisconsin Press, 1967.

Smith, J. L. "Risk Aversion and Bidding Behavior for Offshore Petroleum Leases." *Journal of Industrial Economics* 30 (March 1982):251–69.

Society of Exploration Geophysicists Annual Reports. "Geophysical Activity in 1950–1969." *Geophysics* 17–35 (1951–1970).

Stiglitz, J. E. "The Efficiency of Market Prices in Long Run Allocations in the Oil Industry." In G. M. Brannon, ed., *Studies in Energy Tax Policy*, pp. 55–98. Cambridge, Mass.: Ballinger Publishing Co., 1975.

U. S. Department of the Interior. *Energy Resources on Federally Administered Lands*. Washington, D.C.: Government Printing Office, 1981.

U. S. Department of the Interior, Geological Survey. *Geological Estimates of Undiscovered Recoverable Conventional Resources of Oil and Gas in the United States, A Summary*, Circular 860. Washington, D.C., 1981.

U.S. Department of the Interior, Minerals Management Service. *Federal Offshore Statistics*. Washington, D.C.: Office of Offshore Information Services, Dec. 1975.

———. "Interior Department Announces New OCS Bid Adequacy Procedures." News release. Washington, D.C., 10 March 1983.

———. "Post-Sale Analysis Summary for OCS Sale 69 (Part II)." Sale Specific Data Series 3/Number 4. Gulf of Mexico OCS Region, Metairie, La., 14 March 1983.

———. *Federal Offshore Statistics*. Washington, D.C.: Office of Offshore Information Services, Dec. 1983.

U.S. General Accounting Office, Comptroller General's Report to Congress. *Impact of Regulations—After Federal Leasing—On Outer Continental Shelf Oil and Gas Development*, EMD-81-48. Washington, D.C., 27 Feb. 1981.

———. *Issues in Leasing Offshore Lands for Oil and Gas Development*, EMD-81-59. Washington, D.C., 26 March 1981.

———. *Congress Should Extend Mandate to Experiment with Alternative Bidding Systems in Leasing Offshore Lands*, GAO/RCED-83-139. Washington, D.C., 27 May 1983.

U.S. President, Executive Office of the President, *The National Energy Plan*, 1977.

Weston, J. F., and E. F. Brigham. *Managerial Finance*, 6th ed., pp. 249–82. Hinsdale, Ill.: Dryden Press, 1978.

Wilcox, S. M. "Joint Venture Bidding and Entry in the Market for Offshore Petroleum Leases." Unpublished Ph.D. dissertation, University of California, Santa Barbara, March 1975.

Wilson, R. B. "Competitive Bidding With Asymmetrical Information." *Management Science* 13 (July 1967):816–20.

———. "A Bidding Model of Perfect Competition," *Review of Economic Studies* 44 (1977):511.

INDEX

ABOUT THE AUTHORS

Walter J. Mead is professor of economics at the University of California at Santa Barbara. His extensive research on outer continental shelf issues began with the Public Land Law Review Commission in 1968, and has included studies for the Committee for Economic Development, Stanford Research Institute, the U.S. Forest Service, U.S. Bureau of Land Management, the Federal Trade Commission, U.S. Office of Technology Assessment, Naval Petroleum and Oil Shale Reserve, Alaska Legislature Resources Committee, and Washington State Department of Ecology.

Dr. Mead is a member of the editorial boards of *Industrial Organization Review* and *Land Economics,* and past president of the Western Economic Association. He was senior economist for the Ford Foundation Energy Policy Project (1972–73), and a member of the University of California Council on Energy and Resources (1974–77).

Dr. Mead has authored more than 100 articles and reviews, which have appeared in numerous volumes and such journals as the *American Economic Review, American Journal of Agricultural Economics, Antitrust Bulletin, Contemporary Issues, Current History, The Energy Journal, Forest Science, Journal of Energy and Economic Development, Journal of Forestry, Land Economics, Marine Technology Society, Materials and Society, National Tax Journal, Natural Resources Journal, Public Land Policy, Quarterly of the Colorado School of Mines, Rocky Mountain Mineral Law Journal, Science,* and *Western Economic Journal.*

His books and monographs include *Competition for Federal Timber in the Pacific Northwest* (with T. E. Hamilton), *Competition and Oligopsony in the Douglas Fir Lumber Industry, Mergers and Economic Concentration in the Douglas Fir Lumber Industry, Timber Policy Issues in British Columbia* (coedited with William McKillop), *Transporting Natural Gas From the Arctic: The Alternative Systems,* and *U.S. Energy Policy: Errors of the Past, Proposals for the Future* (coedited with A.E. Utton).

Asbjorn Moseidjord is assistant professor of economics at St. Mary's College of California and West Coast market consultant for the Norwegian Trade Commission. Dr. Moseidjord received his M.A. and Ph.D. degrees in economics from the University of California at Santa Barbara and was senior economist for RECON Research Corporation from 1983 to 1985. His research includes analyses of the economic impact of the Amoco-Cadiz oil spill in 1980, and studies of outer continental shelf oil and gas leases.

Dr. Moseidjord's articles have appeared in *Contemporary Policy Issues, The Energy Journal, The Journal of Energy and Development, Natural Resources Journal, Review of Economics and Statistics,* and *World Oil.*

Dennis D. Muraoka is associate professor of economics at California State University, Long Beach. He received his B.A. in economics and mathematics, his M.A. in urban economics, and his Ph.D. in economics from the University of California at Santa Barbara. Dr. Muraoka has provided economic analysis of municipal and industrial projects concerning natural resources and energy-related issues.

Dr. Muraoka has authored or coauthored articles for professional journals such as *Contemporary Policy Issues, The Energy Journal, National Tax Journal, Natural Resources Journal,* and *Oil and Gas Tax Quarterly,* as well as for several local and federal government publications. He contributed a chapter (with R. B. Watson) to the Pacific Institute book, *Forestlands: Public and Private.*

Philip E. Sorensen received his Ph.D. in economics from the University of California at Berkeley. He is professor of economics at Florida State University and has also taught at the University of California at Santa Barbara, University of California at Berkeley, and Claremont McKenna College. Dr. Sorensen served as chief economist for the California Department of Justice's "Study of the Santa Barbara Oil Spill" (1974–76) and the Commonwealth of Puerto Rico's "Study of the Bahia

Sucia Oil Spill" (1976–79). In addition, he was a member of the Steering Committee of the joint U.S.–French Scientific Research Project on the Cadiz Oil Spill (1978–81), and a member of the Economic Advisory Committee to the Florida Department of Environmental Regulation (1977–present), and the U.S. Delegation to the OECD Conference on Economic Analysis of oil spills (1981).

His articles and reviews have appeared in *The American Journal of Agricultural Economics, The Energy Journal, Land Economics, Marine Resource Economics, National Tax Journal, Natural Resources Journal, Ocean Industry, Oil and Gas Journal, Review of Economics and Statistics,* and *State and Local Government Review.*

Dr. Sorensen is the coauthor of *The California Waste Management Study; Severance Taxes, Royalty Rates, and Leasing Policy Toward Oil and Gas Resources Within State Jurisdiction in the United States; A Comparative Analysis of Alternatives for Limiting Access to Ocean Recreational Salmon Fishing* (with F. Hester); *Competition in OCS Oil and Gas Lease Sales and Lease Development, 1954–1969* (with W. Mead); *Assessing the Economic Damages of Oil Spills: The Amoco-Cadiz Case Study;* and *Cross Subsidization and Competition* (with W. Mead and S. Parsons).